Bless 'em all
Bless 'em all
The long and the short and the tall
Bless all the sergeants and WO1s
Bless all the corporals and their bastard sons
'Cause we're saying goodbye to them all
As back to the barracks we crawl
There'll be no promotion
This side of the ocean
So cheer up my lads, bless 'em all!

For Al Cooper, Eldon Fairburn, Herb Gallifent, Eugene Smith, Reg Starks, William Arnold Steppler, and Jim Williams.

And for Sam Glassford, who died too soon.

The Long
and the Short
and the Tall

An Ordinary Airman's War

Robert Collins

Western Producer Prairie Books
Saskatoon, Saskatchewan

Cover design by Warren Clark/GDL

Printed and bound in Canada

Western Producer Prairie Books is a unique publishing venture located in the middle of western Canada and owned by a group of prairie farmers who are members of Saskatchewan Wheat Pool. From the first book in 1954, a reprint of a serial originally carried in the weekly newspaper *The Western Producer*, to the book before you now, the tradition of providing enjoyable and informative reading for all Canadians is continued.

Canadian Cataloguing in Publication Data

Collins, Robert, 1924-

　The long and the short and the tall

　ISBN 0-88833-187-8

1. Collins, Robert, 1924-　2. World War, 1939-
1945 – Personal narratives, Canadian. 3. Canada.
Royal Canadian Air Force – Airmen – Biography. I. Title.

D811.C44 1986　940.54′4971　C86-098029-4

Preface

This book is not about heroes.

I admire, almost venerate, those Canadians who fought and died at Dieppe and Normandy and Caen; who flew night after night through tracers and flak; who went down in flaming wreckage and choked in oil-slicked seas; who went through hell in Japanese prison camps; who came home maimed of body and mind for the rest of their lives. I envy them a little, in the fruitless way we all wish we had been better than we were.

But they were the glittering minority in World War II. For every hero and heroine there were probably a hundred others in all of the services who—through luck of the draw, lack of initiative, or the nature of their jobs—were not. I was one of those.

RCAF ground crew have been almost ignored in histories of the war because, although their work was vital and some of them died in action, for the most part that work was undramatic. The best available book on the British Commonwealth Air Training Plan is devoted almost exclusively to air crew. It fails to even *mention* the Technical Training Station at St. Thomas, Ontario, where 45,000 ground crew received final training.

But this is a personal memoir, in part a response to those readers of *Butter Down the Well* who have asked what happened to the farm kid from the final page of that book.

What happened to him—though uneventful and unheroic—happened to thousands of others. Here, I hope, other former airmen and airwomen, soldiers, sailors, CWACs and Wrens will recognize a little of their own ordinary war: The great adventure of leaving home for the first time. The heartache of farewells. The silly maddening ways of the military. The waiting, the wasting of time, and, in spite of those things, the secret pride at serving. The journeys to strange and sometimes exciting places. The warmth and endless turnover of friendships. The falling in and out of love. And, in the end, the growing up, in ways that we might never have achieved without the war.

Acknowledgments

"You must have a great memory," said certain readers of *Butter Down the Well* (usually other writers), with overtones of disbelief and sharp insinuating glances. *You made it up, didn't you?* they meant.

But that book and this one are nonfiction, as accurate as memory and research could make them. Here, I triggered recollections partly by retracing some of the steps of forty years ago: the walk from Brandon's CPR station to the former site of No. 2 Manning Depot, the side streets leading from my Moose Jaw boarding house to Wet-Pee, the corridors of TTS, St. Thomas, and the road leading into Wombleton, Yorkshire. My military records from the Public Archives of Canada were invaluable (any veteran can apply for his or hers). Old letters, newspapers, documents and musical recordings, and the recollections of friends all over Canada rounded out the research.

Among those friends, old and new, I owe thanks to Roy Bien, Aiden Cave, Margaret Collins, Charles R. Conacher, Bob Eastman, Eldon Fairburn, Joseph J. Fink, Herb Gallifent, Edna Glassford, Don Gough, Diamond Jim Greer, H. G. Hamilton, E. A. Henry, Norman Ibsen, Wilf Kesterton, William Kondra, Omer Lavallee, Bill Lewis, Lewis "Scoop" Lewry, Fred McGuinness, Bill McVean, Paul Marshall, A. D. Milroy, Roy de Nevers, Colette Nishizaki, Yvonne and Russ Pettigrew, Al Powell, Homer Rourke, Hugh Sims, Reg Starks, William Arnold Steppler, Doug Steubing, Jack Taylor, Marty Waddell, and Margaret Winters.

The staffs of the Elgin Military Museum, St. Thomas; the Directorate of History, Department of National Defence, Ottawa; the Provincial Archives of Saskatchewan; the Maritime Museum, Toronto; and the Commonwealth Air Training Plan Museum, Brandon, generously shared their time and facilities. A. E. Karlen of the Royal Canadian Air Force Association in Ottawa and, particularly, J. A. Waschuk in Saskatoon were helpful in my search for former RCAF friends. The Department of National Defence, through Associate Minister Harvie Andre, supplied useful facts.

My daughter Lesley helped with research, as did Debra Hebb, and provided many fresh tuna sandwiches during the writing. My daughter Catherine, managing editor of The Financial Post *Moneywise Magazine*, was my first editor, and a superb one. My thanks to the publisher who coaxed and encouraged me from the idea four years ago to its conclusion.

Chapter One

Never in my life have I been in such a motley crowd—or felt so totally alone.

I am surrounded by 750 naked and half-naked men. Skinny men, plump men, Greek gods. Men in boxer shorts, dirty shorts, and no shorts. Men with body odor that would fell an ox. Men brooding silently on their bunks. Men shouting, laughing, punching biceps, breaking wind, cursing, telling world-class dirty jokes that would leave the wise guys propped up outside the pool hall back home mute with awe and admiration.

Apart from a nodding acquaintance with an acne-ridden Toronto youth across the aisle, who proudly informs me that he's had syphilis three times (I am very careful not to shake hands), I know none of these people.

It is 10 P.M., September 11, 1943, bedtime at No. 2 Manning Depot in the bowels of the Brandon Winter Fair building, commonly known as the Horse Palace. My first great adventure is beginning to seem like a terrible mistake. What am I doing here? What madness made me leave my safe and gentle Saskatchewan home for this *barn* full of rude, nude, raucous strangers?

I have been in His Majesty's Royal Canadian Air Force precisely thirty-six hours and here at Manning a mere six. But already my mother, father, and brother, and the farmhouse where I have lived for all of my nineteen years, seem lost forever, beloved but distant as a dream. Where are those long-awaited pleasures of being an airman? Where are those handsome laughing fellows from the recruiting posters, in tailor-made uniforms with wings on their chests, beneath the seductive words "WORLD TRAVELER AT 21"? The posters never mentioned the Horse Palace.

In peacetime this building housed prize-winning horses and

1

cattle. The troughs for flushing away their manure are still molded into the gray cement floor a few inches below my head. *Is the air force trying to tell me something?* So far, we have moved in herds, like Old Reddy and Whiteface and the other cows back home. Nobody has made me feel welcome or wanted. I am scared, confused, exhilarated by turns.

We fifteen hundred new and fairly new recruits are bedded down on two floors, among infinite vistas of double-decker metal bunks. We are a cross-country sampler: the air force ships its basic trainees to wherever there's room in one of the four Mannings — Brandon, Toronto, Edmonton, or Lachine, Quebec. There are *Easterners* among us — a rare exotic species. I've never really known an Easterner. Will they be snobs? bullies? smarter than me? For the moment that's irrelevant. What matters is that I and five other pieces of human raw material who shambled off the train this Saturday afternoon are the newest, rawest, and greenest of all.

We have no uniforms yet — the Depot stores are closed. Not only are we *visibly* new, but our clothes betray our backgrounds. Mine — a cheap somber brown suit, the only one I own, and a salt-and-pepper cloth cap — say "rural hick." Or so I *think*, which is all that matters tonight.

Earlier this evening, in our telltale civvies, we stepped timidly into the vast mess hall. I had never before been to a cafeteria or even a summer camp. I had eaten *en masse* only at rural schoolhouse socials or at my mother's dinner table with ten or twelve other men at threshing time. In those places, the menfolk sat stuffing their faces while the womenfolk eagerly served them.

Here, we tentatively followed the leader to trays, plates, cutlery, down a long line of steam tables and kettles where indifferent airmen in white ladled out — what? Stew maybe. Plentiful and probably nourishing, but bland and anonymous. Fleetingly, I longed for my mother's roast chicken, served on her dinnerware with the little primroses around the edges that I'd eaten from all my life. I read the derision in the mess crew's eyes: *Better get used to it, airman, your mommy ain't waiting on you now.*

We huddled at long trestle tables in the perpetual din — loud voices, clashing cutlery, shouts from the kitchen — not quite finishing our food. The uniforms around us gulped their meals like boa constrictors (they never seemed to *chew*) and we didn't want to be different. Afterward, just time to get blankets and sheets — *You bastards are lucky; the army don't get sheets!* Then, into this sea of humanity, the Horse Palace.

Everything is huge, chaotic, astonishing. And as on all first-days in life—first-day-at-school, first-day-at-camp, first-day-in-new-church, first-day-at-the-office—we know, we are *certain*, that all the others are watching us, measuring us, laughing at us. Now, thank God it is bedtime. Surely tomorrow we'll get uniforms and blend in?

The lights are out. The great echoing room is subsiding, like a large beast that has turned around three times in the weeds and curled up for the night. In my whole life I have never slept in a room with more than one other person—the cubicle of a bedroom I shared with my younger brother, Larry, with only the sighing of wind through the poplar tree belt, or a coyote somewhere far out in the stubble, or the welcome boom of thunder that meant the end of drought, or on winter nights the eerie hum of frost-caked telephone lines, singing-singing-singing.

Gradually my nerve ends stop jangling and then . . . a piercing cry:

"FUCK THE EAST!"

And instantly, as though on cue:

"FUCK THE WEST!"

And others take up the chorus, a cacaphony of ribald shouts ricocheting off the cement floor, the high ceiling, the metal bunks. *What's going on!*

Sure, I know there is East-West rivalry. All of us from Saskatchewan routinely hate Toronto, knowing with sweet certainty that it is rich, privileged, and scornful of us stubble-jumpers. We graduates of the Depression remember the boxcars of free Ontario food and clothing with mixed gratitude and resentment. *Charity from the East!* None of us can forget the carloads of Maritimes dried codfish, sent with good intentions—and the texture and taste of salted boot leather. But even so . . .

And that *word!* Even my father, a virtuoso swearer with a wide repertoire, never used the f-word. My mother, a devout church-goer, never said anything stronger than "darn." Even at school the *word* was used only sparingly, by really bad boys, the kind your mother said you mustn't play with. And then only in huddled dirty talk behind the horse barn, the rest of us listening wide-eyed while the girls, ears straining, hovered watchfully on our periphery, hoping for something incriminating to report to the teacher . . .

But now a weary voice, maybe a corporal's, cuts through the racket.

3

"*AWRIGHT,* you bastards!"

The room settles down again with sighs and snorts and chuckles and mutterings and comfortable grunts. Now I understand. This is a nightly ritual. It is our bedtime story. For the first time I feel a hint of belonging to . . . *something.*

Nothing dramatic or heroic like standing shoulder to shoulder to fight Hitler. Most of us *are* here for patriotic reasons but we would never admit to it in this company of strangers. At this moment we are far from the hated enemy and may never lay eyes on him.

No, our adversaries, for now, are the system that already has turned us into numbers and is about to mold us into marching machines, and the corporals and sergeants who will strive to maintain their proud reputations as mean sons of bitches. Already I sense the adversary system: from the noncommissioned officers strutting around this barn and from the cynical gibes of recruits who've been here three or four days. Already we are united against It and Them, and against our loneliness and apprehension. It is a scrap of comfort at the end of a bewildering day.

I huddled wakefully that first night between the coarse sheets and the gray blanket, with a strange body heaving and snoring in the upper bunk overhead. A kaleidoscope of thoughts and memories whirled through my mind. Why *was* I here?

That was easy. Partly because, a generation before, a short feisty red-headed Belfast-born English-raised patriot named John Douglas Collins—my father—had left his newly acquired Saskatchewan homestead the moment World War I was declared, joined the Lord Strathcona Horse cavalry regiment, gone overseas with the first Canadian contingent, and the following spring marched into the front lines of France, *sans* horse, like the rest of his regiment.

In the autumn he was carried out of the melee of that war, sick and bloated: from the late-spring Battle of Festubert; from a summer of lice and mud and relentless shellfire; from poison gas and the inhuman trenches. After a long convalescence in England they sent him home, with orders to work outdoors if he wanted to stay alive. He went back to farming on his 320 southern Saskatchewan acres, five miles south of the village of Shamrock. He was a literate man with a profound distrust of things mechanical. He'd have been ill-suited for farming, even

4

with good health. Now a friend met him at the train, looked at his face, aged and wrinkled before its time, and wept.

"My God, Jack," he said brokenly. "What have they *done* to you!"

My father's war was over then—except it never really ended. Its physical ills and bad memories plagued him for life. He rarely talked about it, and never with the affection and nostalgia of many veterans. But one day, when my brother and I were small, we coaxed him to show us how a cavalryman rode. He was then in his fifties, cursed with lumbago, but he vaulted on and off our bemused saddle horse and cantered her around the farmyard sitting straight as an arrow, to our total delight, and his.

Sometimes he would snap us a salute and we'd snap one back, everyone laughing. And once, shortly before he died in the Vancouver veterans' hospital in 1957 of age and the residual damage of the war, he confusedly barked out military commands from forty-two years before. That day, no one laughed.

Despite what the war did to him, his patriotism never wavered. He believed in the Royal Family and the Empire as fervently as he despised Canadian prime minister William Lyon Mackenzie King, the Liberal party, and socialism. When World War II broke out, he wanted to enlist, which would have been laughable had he not been in deadly earnest. He was far too old and frail to serve even in the Veterans' Guard at such tasks as guarding prison camps.

He, and we, listened to the radio war news several times a day. We sat hushed and reverent when Winston Churchill's fighting speeches crackled through from London. Once Churchill visited Ottawa, spoke to Parliament, and derisively told how the boastful Hitler had threatened to wring England's neck like a chicken's.

"Some chicken! . . ." Churchill's voice rang over the airwaves, and in our living room we joined in the gales of laughter from the MPs and senators. And then, with his impeccable timing, ". . . Some neck!" I would gladly have risen up and marched to battle beside Churchill that day.

I clipped maps from the Regina *Leader-Post*, charting every rise and fall of Allied fortunes. There was no way that Jack Collins' oldest son could not have red-white-and-blue coursing through his veins. My father never urged me to enlist; I think he dreaded it. He knew more about war than most men in our neighborhood (few were veterans). But I owed it to him. I knew that if I joined up he would be burstingly proud. And he was.

It was not *just* my father's influence and example. My family

5

and most of our neighbors were caught up in the drama and adventure of World War II. We were certain that it was a just war. Hitler had forced it so we were going to beat him. There was urgency and camaraderie in the air. You gave blood to help a wounded soldier. You dropped coins into milk bottles on grocery store counters to buy "Milk for Britain." Anyone who did not buy Victory Bonds was practically an ally of the Axis (Germany, Italy, and Japan). You could begin with a twenty-five–cent War Savings Stamp; sixteen of them bought a five-dollar War Savings Certificate. These paid 3.21 percent over 7½ years, which seemed eminently fair to us.

We salvaged everything. Old pots and pans, toothpaste tubes and the tinfoil wrappings from cigarette packages, for their aluminum. Leftover fat, for the glycerine in high explosives. My school friend Mac Smart and I canvassed local farms for rusting and abandoned machinery, lugged back-breaking tons of it into a truck, and sold it to make guns or God-knew-what, loyally donating the money—about six thousand cigarettes' worth—to the cigarette fund, an endless tide of nicotine for our fighting men.

Food, gasoline, beer, and hard liquor were rationed. None of this much mattered to us: we grew most of our food, rarely drove our 1929 Chev, and never let booze pass our lips. (My mother abhorred it and my father abstained because of his health.) But being rationed made us feel closer to the war afar.

The radio, newspaper, and magazines brought that distant war into Shamrock. I saw photos of overalled women in munitions factories, their curls tied up in head scarves, never dreaming that I was witnessing women's liberation. Advertisements showed little girls with fingers to lips cautioning, "Please! A War Worker Is Sleeping." The radio played "Milkman, Keep Those Bottles Quiet" and "When the Lights Go On Again" and we sang along, although I'd never seen a milkman or a blackout. As an ardent do-it-yourselfer, patching things around the farm with baling wire and ingenuity, I read with pleasure of a soldier in North Africa who pressed his pants by laying them between two boards and driving a jeep over them.

All around us young men and women were trickling into the forces. Big husky Roland Hook, from a couple of miles south, joined the army and the fighting in Europe. Handsome swarthy Earl Brown joined the air force and lost his life on a mission—not so long after our school played softball against his. My cousin Dora enlisted in the RCAF Women's Division. My high school friends, the inseparable Henry twins, separated to join the navy and the army. I was not about to be left out.

With my father's health failing, I could have opted to be an essential farm worker, exempt from military service, as many friends did. But I would have been a terrible farmer. I was a bookish, skinny, unathletic scarecrow, not much good at anything except school. I loved the land but I wanted to be a writer.

This didn't make me a Grade A candidate for soldiering. Nor was I brave, but bravery or lack of it was almost incidental. Given the mood of the times, it took more courage to stay home. One young neighbor—a kind, polite, hard-working fellow several years older than I (he'd kept a watchful eye over me in my first year at grade school)—went to jail rather than abandon his religious principles about war. It caused a flurry of oohs and ahhs over the party line. I knew he was not a coward, but others didn't. Why didn't he go to war like everyone else? they whispered.

The war was duty but also high romance, and the RCAF was the newest, most glamorous of the services. Everything exciting seemed to be happening in the air. My father's nightmare in the trenches had soured me on the army. The navy seemed a bad bet because I couldn't swim. But the air force! Harvard and Anson and Tiger Moth trainers from air bases at Mossbank or Moose Jaw sometimes flew over our fields. I craned my neck at them, awed and wistful.

Most important, my special pal Roy Bien was already a wireless air gunner. To me, it was the ultimate in glamor: he manned the guns in battle and at other times operated that fascinating instrument the wireless radio. He was three years older but we had often walked home together from grade school. I hero-worshiped him—the way he danced, played the guitar and yodeled, got the girls. When he came home on leave with the WAG's white half-wing on his blue chest, I was consumed with envy. It *had* to be the air force.

All of this was impossible to put into coherent words. Not yet eighteen when I finished grade twelve—the end of high school in Saskatchewan—I mumbled to my parents, "Guess I'll be joining up soon."

My father nodded. "I guess we knew you would."

My mother, looking fixedly at her sewing, said quietly, "What would you do, Son?"

"Something like what Roy's doing."

None of us said much more at the time. My mother's face was

taut and troubled. It was not that we expected me to die in battle (few who joined up *expected* it). It was simply that our little foursome was breaking up. We had done everything together as a family. Even in the depths of the Depression, there had been a comforting sameness and unity to our lives. Now nothing would ever be the same again.

That summer my father had a chance for easier work, managing Shamrock's lumberyard. The wheat and oats that summer of 1942 were the best we'd seen in years. He took the job and I promised to stay on long enough to help harvest the crop. An early autumn snow caught the stooks I had made before we could thresh them. Through that fall and winter I ran the farm and all its livestock reasonably well, with my mother and brother's help. In the spring we belatedly threshed, then arranged to rent the place to neighbor Tommy Hawkins. Then it was definitely time to go to war. Roy Bien had just gone overseas.

Armed with air force recruiting literature, I hitched a ride to Moose Jaw, sixty miles from home, with Tim Adams, the gentle cultured Englishman who ran our village post office. Mister Adams, as we boys were taught to address him, knew everything about the world, or so I thought. For my first night ever in a hotel he recommended the respectable Harwood. Its advertisement tantalized with "110 rooms, 35 with bath, every guest room with own private toilet; soft water" for $1.50 single.

The next morning I presented myself to the RCAF in the Hammond Building on Main Street. They languidly filled out forms and instructed me to report to No. 5 Recruiting Centre in Regina two weeks later. Those two trips set a new record for personal travel: until then I'd been on a train and in a city only once.

The Regina recruiters were equally unmoved by my presence. By 1943 the air force had plenty of applicants, and I was no bargain. My medical exam proved me basically sound, although more like a famine victim than the handsome hunks in the recruiting posters: five-foot-eleven in my bare bony feet, 125 pounds with a thirty-one–inch chest and sparrows' ankles.

Then they handed me the color-vision test—pages of bewildering colored dots that revealed certain numerals to the medically fit. I saw *no* numbers, or the wrong ones. I was blue-green color blind! "Definitely unsafe," said the medical officer, for air crew or any ground duty involving colored wiring or lights.

I was stunned, flabbergasted, desperate. I could not be like Roy Bien. I could not even learn radio, which was part of my

8

dream. The air force was yanking everything out from under me. I'd had no inkling of faulty color vision. I could tell red from green from blue! But because they said I couldn't, the only options were cook or airframe mechanic. A *cook?* I could never face Roy again.

Yet it *had* to be the air force. Airframe mechanic was acceptable; it meant tinkering with all parts of a plane except the engine. As a farm tinkerer I reckoned I could cope with that. They gave me a mechanical aptitude test. I scored thirty out of a hundred. A corporal gazed at my score in disbelief.

"Sure you don't wanna be a cook, kid?" he said.

But a Flight Lieutenant W. C. Cumming was more charitable when he saw my high school marks. My wonderful grade twelve teacher, Richard Schmalenberg, had coached and inspired me to a strong finish: a 78.4 percent average including, predictably, A's in literature and composition and, unpredictably, more A's in the subjects I hated—trigonometry, chemistry, and geometry.

Cumming also liked my Classification Test score. The CT, which the air force used to assess "basic intellectual suitability," covered eighty points of mental ability, ranging through perceptual alertness, numbers sense, following directions, verbal sense, and reasoning ability. In the thirty-minute time limit I scored seventy-one out of eighty, about twenty more than the average high school graduate.

"An above average rural lad—intelligent, cooperative," Cumming wrote on my form. "While MAT [mechanical aptitude] score is low, CT is high and has a good academic record. Believe he is well worth a try."

So I was accepted. Still smarting from rejection, I begged a different color test for a week later. At home during the interim, my peaceable mother turned into a tiger. How *dare* the air force say her boy was defective! But back in Regina the results, retested with pinpoint colored lights, were the same.

"Go home and finish the harvest; you'll be needed there," the recruiters said soothingly. "Report to Brandon Manning Pool in the fall."

Being an intelligent, cooperative rural lad, I did. I stooked more grain, pitched more sheaves, and wondered, with mingled glee and fear, what was ahead.

Then, one crisp September morning, I left my mother in tears beside the big flat stone that was the back doorstep at our farmhouse. She who had stayed cheerful through a life of hard times. She of that strong stoic God-fearing Pennsylvania-Dutch stock named Hartzell. She who'd grown up on a hard-scrabble North Dakota farm, won a scholarship to university but never had a chance to use it, begun teaching at eighteen to help support her mother, and met Jack Collins, the love of her life, during a classroom stint in Saskatchewan. All through the awful years of the Depression, all through dust and grasshoppers and no crops and no money, I'd seen her cry only once before.

I left my father at Shamrock's depot, a carbon copy of all the little dull-red clapboard CPR depots across Canada. He was an articulate man, and never ashamed to show emotion, but this moment was too painful for both of us. We gripped hands, hard. He squeezed my shoulder once. We murmured words. The train jerked away. I looked back, with an ache in my throat. He stood rigid on the wooden platform, his shoulders a little slumped, his normally cheerful face set grim and valiant.

In Regina the next day (by chance, it was my nineteenth birthday) I stood with a handful of others before the Red Ensign and intoned, "I, Robert John Collins, do sincerely promise and swear that I will be faithful and bear true allegiance to His Majesty." Now until war's end I would be R270747, Collins, R. J.

The next morning I boarded the 8:55 CPR mainline train for Manitoba, clutching two military meal tickets entitling me to breakfast and lunch. When I laid out a ticket after my first ever meal in a dining car the steward sighed noisily and raised his eyes heavenward. *Oh-Lord-why-have-you-sent-your-humble-servant-this-miserable-wretch?*

"You shoulda given me that *before* you ordered," he scolded. This traveler was just another dumb recruit, he realized, so the chances of a tip were nil.

Then getting off at Brandon, a whole *province* away, clinging to my father's worn black club bag, I gravitated uncertainly to a sign at the end of the platform: AIRFORCE RECRUITS ASSEMBLE HERE. A corporal scooped me up with five other lost souls. "Awright, you men, follow me!" Bored with his menial task and not bothering to try *marching* the likes of us, he led us in a straggle up the steps to Pacific Avenue and a half-mile straight up Tenth Street.

Passersby scarcely gave us a glance; the little city was teeming with airmen. In ten minutes we crossed Victoria Avenue to the ornate front of the Arena and Winter Fair building—two storeys and a great arched roof with long deep windows, my first of many homes-away-from-home. As we filed timidly past the armed sentries into its enormous maw, a few blue-uniformed airmen chanted, "You'll be sorr-eee!" We smiled weakly, sensing correctly that it was a standing joke, a mandatory warning for all newcomers. It was a chant I'd hear often in the years ahead but it seemed especially apt this night. . . .

But now as I finally fall asleep in the Horse Palace there is one bright memory of humanity amidst the chaos. As we readied ourselves for bed, we newcomers fumbling through the unfamiliar routine—*Which way to the john? Does anybody brush his teeth? Where do you put your clothes? Does anybody wear pajamas?* (most men slept in their underwear, or nothing)—a young man with a long lean face and prominent nose dropped to his knees just before lights out, folded his hands, bowed his head, and silently prayed.

My heart went out to him. I had not been taught to pray beside my bed so had no need to test my convictions now, but I would never have had the guts to do it in this crowd of noisy profane strangers. There were a few sidelong glances, grins, winks, a surreptitious whisper or two, but no one baited him.

His courage of conviction that first night was a good thought to go to sleep on.

Chapter Two

For six weeks the rest of the world melted from sight. Our world was this place, its newness, its stifling regulations, its little humiliations. We were *in* the war but knew virtually nothing *about* it.

At home my family and I had listened to the radio news four or five times a day. I read the Regina *Leader-Post* in bunches, brought twice weekly by the branch line. In the weekly current events contest at Shamrock high school, I won enough War Savings Coupons to buy a five-dollar War Savings Bond. I knew almost as much about the war as Hitler and probably more than Mackenzie King.

Yet now, although a half-step closer to it, I hadn't the faintest notion what was happening out there. The western Allies were battling for Salerno, the Russians had retaken Smolensk; but I saw no newspapers, heard no radio. We were not forbidden to read or listen. Our days were simply filled with one concern: staying alive, in the trainees' sense; keeping one jump ahead of the corporals; keeping the sergeants off our backs; avoiding such dreaded penalties as a couple of days in the digger (detention) – a fear that the NCOs craftily nurtured in us. Far too late, we realized that the digger was reserved for really serious stuff, such as striking an officer or seducing the camp commander's wife.

I had come from a home of "Please," "Thank you," and "You're welcome." Here, the common form of address was a shouted order, threat, or reprimand: to straighten your back, suck in your gut, "get cracking," or "get the lead out." Malingering was "swingin' the lead" or "fuggin' the dog." It covered such minor sins as faking the pushups in P.T. or reporting sick with imaginary ills. The penalty could be a "joe-job": washing dishes, scrubbing latrines, picking litter off the ground – any grubby menial task the NCOs in their infinite creativity could dream up. A man could also be "joe'd" by pure bad luck—being the first one in a sergeant's line of vision when a dirty job needed doing or having a name that began with *A* instead of *Z*.

In the semantic sense, we never *went* anywhere; we "paraded." A parade was rarely a triumphant march to brass bands and cheering crowds. It was a lineup. "Pay parade" meant lining up for money. "Sick parade" meant waiting in line for an aspirin and a warning about swingin' the lead.

For eight days we went nowhere in the literal sense either. New arrivals were held in Reception Wing—a state of mind, not location—and strictly confined to barracks. Not once did we step outdoors. Our boundaries were brown metal bunks, gray cement floors, waves of blue uniforms, a monochrome world.

On the first Monday morning, things had begun to happen. We Saturday night latecomers were herded into Equipment and Clothing Stores and laden with "kit": three pairs of black socks, two baggy undershorts, four blue shirts, one collar pin, black necktie, fatigues, two blue uniforms. Blue wedge cap. Bowl-shaped winter cap with tie-up–fold-down ear flaps, despised by us all and forever known as the "Piss Pot." A great thumping pair of black boots. A holdall for brushes and razor, and a "housewife" mending kit. Black leather gloves. Blue raincoat; rubber ground-sheet. Finally the "greatcoat, airman-for-the-use-of," with shawl collar and vast lapels.

The airmen in Stores were pleased to have a new audience for their old jokes. "All clothes that fit, bring 'em back!" they cried merrily. Much of it *didn't* fit—it had been manufactured for tribes of giants and pygmies—but the air force was unperturbed. There *was* a tailor shop for emergencies: fitting grotesquely misshapen uniforms to similarly misshapen men. For minor looseness or long sleeves, Stores said cheerfully, "You'll fill out!" They sounded like my mother.

A few big-city Beau Brummels, pining for the twenty-two–inch flared cuffs they'd left behind on civvy street, slipped into a downtown tailor at the first opportunity to have gussets sewn in. A flight sergeant cut the miscreants down to size the next morning on parade, and their pants quickly followed suit.

Everything itched. The thick new trousers chafed my thighs and grabbed at my crotch. The cap rasped my forehead. But in time, the woolly fabric would wear down to a tough smooth nap *almost* like the officers' (theirs, of course, was a different blue and of superior material).

Scratchy or not, there have been few moments in life to match the elation I felt, getting into that uniform for the first time. I knotted the tie in the too-big collar around my scrawny neck, tightened the belt around my wasp-waist, set the wedge cap at a jaunty angle two fingers' width over the right eye. The image in the washroom mirror looked *almost* like the recruiting posters. My visible past had vanished! I looked like everyone else. I was an *airman*.

In the barbershop Jack Taylor and his three helpers, who trimmed tens of thousands of rookie heads through all the years of No. 2 Manning, sheared us according to regulation: no hair more than 1½ inches long. Our ears sprang into view beside skin that had never seen the light of day. Barbers ran *their* old jokes past us:

"You wanta keep your sideburns?"

"Yeah, sure!"

"Okay . . . [handing them over] . . . here y'are!"

Taylor, a fatherly fellow of nearly fifty, asked us all to sign his autograph books. Forty years later he turned them over to Brandon's air force museum where I found my spidery signature and those of a score of friends—eerie echoes of the past. Ginger-haired E. P. Aseltine from Pine Falls, Manitoba, his droll eyes promising mischief. Al Cooper from Winnipeg, short and frail looking, with a wide smile and a quick sense of humor. Big hearty Bob Sisterson, another Winnipegger, mustached, older (probably all of twenty-six!), and seemingly at ease in this alien environment. Errol Hill, blonde and dashing, from Port Arthur. Mike Melnick, a solid billet of a boy from Cobalt, Ontario.

Friendships were the redeeming part of those strange early days. Here there was always someone to appreciate my sense of humor (which leaned towards P. G. Wodehouse and radio's Fred Allen, rather than Red Skelton or Laurel and Hardy). And here I was finally fathoming the mysterious East. To that point I had met maybe four Easterners—two loquacious Ontario boys working the prairie harvest one autumn and two pretty, self-assured girls operating an Anglican Church Sunday school van one summer. Paralyzingly shy myself, I'd assumed all Easterners were sophisticated and blessed with the gift of gab. Now I knew they weren't—and that all Torontonians did not have horns and forked tails. Here, sharing this grand adventure and that great equalizer,

14

the uniform, most of them seemed much like me. It was a valuable boost for my self-esteem.

At first I gravitated to other farm and small-town boys, whether from East or West. One was Norm McParland, the devout Catholic who'd prayed beside his bunk that first night. We were fairly dissimilar—he was lean and hard of body, a product of northern Ontario's hard-rock mining country, not a man to mess with—but we shared a basic courtesy and a distaste for blowhards.

My best friend and constant companion was Sam Glassford—initially because he had the neighboring bunk. But we'd have sought each other out, sooner or later. Like me, he had grown up on a farm (at New Liskeard, Ontario), was not afraid of work, and was basically good-natured. He was a rangy deep-chested six-footer, especially strong in the shoulders and arms as more than one playful wrestler found out. Nobody pushed him around, but Sam's disposition was sunny. His lean face with its pointed chin and high cheekbones radiated a V of good cheer, even when we all joined in the mandatory cussing of the system.

Often he called me "Lad." Most of us *were* lads to him: he turned twenty-eight that autumn, nine or ten years older than the majority. He was married, with a three-year-old son and a two-year-old daughter back in Timmins. During the Depression, the annealing of many an adult, he'd worked as a plant operator for Northern Power, an Ontario hydroelectric company. He'd lived among men in groups, which gave him an edge on the likes of me. I think he saw in me a kind of younger brother who needed looking after.

In fact, I was coping better than I'd dared hope after that first daunting night. My latent curiosity—there was more in me than I'd realized—thrived on the new experience. I loved to learn, and there was no shortage of lessons. Nor was there time for homesickness or boredom. In that first week we were inundated with lectures on barracks routine, the training to come, RCAF history, discipline, sanitation and hygiene, badges of rank, how to address an officer, and how to dress ourselves.

The padre and the CO gave us pep talks. The dentist peered into my mouth, then invited several interested colleagues to have a look. My farm diet—lots of vegetables, chewy meat, and little candy—and our "hard" water from deep in the earth, laced with minerals that left a scale on pots and pans, had given me nearly perfect teeth. I soon put a stop to that. Unlimited access to soft drinks and chocolate bars in the canteen gave me cavities like normal folk.

We learned that DROs were "Daily Routine Orders," SSOs were "Station Standing Orders," and SPs were Service Police (equivalent to the army's Military Police), mean and nasty, feared and hated by all but their mothers and wives. We learned we were aircraftmen second class, AC2s, "acey-deucys," "erks," the bottom of the barrel, the lowest form of human life. Above us in the pecking order were AC1s, LACs (leading aircraftmen), corporals, sergeants, flight-sergeants, warrant officers second class, and warrant officers first class.

You could call a flight sergeant "Flight" but a WO1 or WO2 was "Sir." Yet, in one of the RCAF's many paradoxes, warrant officers were not commissioned and not to be saluted. Salutes were reserved for pilot officers, flying officers, flight lieutenants, squadron leaders, and so on into the stratosphere.

We learned that noncommissioned officers (NCOs) would cling to us like barnacles for the rest of our air force lives. One of them, drawing from the long-winded *Manual of RCAF Drill and Ceremonial*, now showed us how to snap a salute. We were to rev up thirty paces before reaching the target, looking the officer "full in the face as much as possible without turning head more than 45 degrees in the required direction." As he (or she, for there *were* women officers, which shook us to the depths of our chauvinistic souls) drew near, we were to extend the right arm horizontally, bring the hand in smartly to the head in a circular motion, slightly higher than and to the right of the right eye. "Upper arm and hand to be straight and elbow in line with level of shoulders, then cut hand and arm smartly down to side and turn head and eyes smartly to the front."

It was a lot of memory work to pack into our tiny brains, but while the novelty lasted we saluted everything that moved. Air crew officers, slightly embarrassed by our zeal, tossed back sloppy casual salutes. Administration brass hats, a different breed, *expected* us to touch our forelocks. Much later, when we discovered that officers were somewhat less than gods, we went to considerable lengths to avoid meeting one, much less saluting one.

Reeling under this information overload, I was too bewildered to care about the forbidden mysteries and delights of Brandon. Manning Depot, a town in itself, filling most of a block between Tenth and Eleventh streets and Victoria and McTavish avenues, had everything we needed. This sprawling place could have swallowed up the entire business section of downtown Shamrock. It was *so* big that the twenty-five–cent *Pocket Guide for Trainees* included a detailed map of the premises.

In my time, Manning held 1,500 trainees and 363 RCAF and civilian staff. The arena portion was nearly a half-century old. Early in World War I it had served first as a temporary mental hospital when the real one burned down, then as an aliens' detention center. So, with the Winter Fair buildings adjoining, we were housed and trained—as we never tired of telling one another—in a place once inhabited by prisoners, beasts, and the insane.

The arena proper was now administration offices, storerooms, detention rooms, and barbershop, all surrounding a central parade square under the soaring domed roof, where once the Brandon Wheat Kings hockey team and various prize Herefords had strutted their stuff. There were also a dry (no booze) canteen, a nine-wicket post office, and a rec room with billiards, ping-pong, and a library.

The barns were a two-storey barracks. We dined in the former chicken house next door. Great-great-grandchildren of its former occupants were often featured on the menu, along with meatballs, macaroni and cheese, and the ever-popular liver and bacon. When in doubt, the cooks creamed the main course, disguising a multitude of sins and errors.

Manning was daunting and impersonal. There was *no* place to be alone. Even the toilets had no doors—a staggering blow to my sense of privacy. So maybe I was a country bumpkin, but what kind of barbarians advertised their bowel movements? Even our outdoor one-holer back on the farm had a *door!* Perhaps it was the military way of discouraging dark deeds between consenting adults. (But if there were gays among us, our merciless banter about "queers," "fruits," and "You guys been playin' drop-the-soap in the shower?" kept them permanently in the closet. Although eagerly joining in the ribald jeers, I wasn't quite sure what a homosexual *was*.) After a few uneasy mornings, joining orderly rows of other men emptying their bowels in full view, I came to accept it as a matter of course.

I had never used a shower before. It was a distinct improvement over the galvanized tub beside our kitchen stove at home. But, with my gentle upbringing, it took a certain plucking-up of nerve to get under the communal spray, elbow to elbow with a dozen mother-naked strangers, our genitals all dangling in the dawn.

I was ashamed of my body. My face was speckled with galloping acne. My arms and legs were like pipe cleaners. I was a dead ringer for the "98-pound weakling" in a contemporary Charles Atlas body-building advertisement: a puny wretch who always got sand kicked in his face by big guys on the beach, and always lost the girl.

Everyone around me seemed muscular and normal. With an innate flair for masochism, I made friends with well-built men who had outgrown their pimples. One amiable blond Viking, from what is now Thunder Bay, had a flawless physique and a sculpted profile like the figurehead on an ancient sailing ship. In the showers, he revealed a member so upstanding, so perfect like the rest of him, that he was instantly nicknamed Knurled Knob (which we, in what passed for wit, pronounced with a hard *K*: Kuh-nurled Kuh-nob). He regarded the name and his appendage with equal pride and affection.

Whatever was left of my native modesty went down the drain at my first RCAF medical. Milling around in the buff in a room packed with other naked men, you wondered what to do with your hands. You joined in nervous bawdy jokes to cover your nakedness of body and spirit ("hey you guys, welcome to the cop shop; this is where all the dicks hang out"). You made mock grabs at your neighbor's crotch, yelling "Cough!", which was what the medical officer said when applying his practised hand to your groin in search of hernia.

It was a time of discovering who had muscles and who didn't, who (like Kuh-nurled Kuh-nob) was "well-hung" or wasn't, who bathed regularly and who didn't. One man smelled *so* bad—maybe it was his terror seeping out—that I remember his acrid odor to this day. There was always an island of space around him.

The MO and his minions did their job with rough efficiency. On the first day they hit us with a smallpox vaccination, a Dick Test for scarlet fever, a Schick Test for diphtheria, a Wasserman Test for VD, and the first of three TABT (typhoid and lockjaw) shots. The fear of needles sent some airmen into a dead faint, and the actual TABT left our arms so swollen that the air force automatically gave us twenty-four hours off.

The medics likewise terrified us with words like "syph," "clap," "dose," and "crabs." They told in gruesome detail how venereal disease would ravage our nether regions. They showed pictures, in lurid color, of VD victims whose precious jewels were flaming red or in advanced states of decay.

But the most shocking and humiliating moment by far was short-arm inspection. "Short-arm" was the armed forces' official euphemism for penis. You lined up with your fellows by the score, unbuttoned your fly (no zippers in those days) if you were so lucky as to be wearing pants at the time, and held your private parts at the ready.

As you rounded in front of the medical officer and his grinning orderly you whipped out and presented your penis. "SQUEEZE!" urged the orderly, to us reluctant and bewildered ones. With a weary glance the MO checked for chancre, discharge, rash, or other evidence of foul disease.

At the first short-arm, I couldn't believe it was happening. We were on the indoor parade square, surrounded by tiers of seats from its previous incarnation as an arena. As I shuffled in line, face flaming, I glanced up in the stands. A couple of WDs (RCAF Women's Division), high in the cheap seats, were looking down with amused smiles. Given our mass embarrassment, they wouldn't have seen much even at arm's length, but it was the final indignity.

There was still more, but nothing as bad as the abominable short-arm. Before that week in Reception Wing ended, thirty-eight of us were assigned to a "flight" (squad) for the duration of Manning: Flight 197. We were photographed and fingerprinted for an ID card, and given dog tags to hang around our necks. We filled out forms, stating our prewar occupations and postwar hopes. I wrote "newspaper reporter or radio announcer."

Last but far from least, we called on the paymaster. As AC2s, we rated $1.30 a day. With my first pay I rushed to the canteen and bought a money belt to carry my pittance, because everyone else was doing it. The money seemed great to me: $39 to $40 a month, $474.50 a year, more than double my father's war disability pension and as much as the farm paid us in the best year of the Depression. The regulations added that if I were admitted to hospital with alcoholism my pay would stop, but if I went in with venereal disease I would lose only seventy-five cents a day.

Clearly, I reflected, as we braced ourselves for Training Wing, it was better to be a lover than a drinker in the RCAF.

Chapter Three

Hahbout–TUH! . . . Byyy the Lef', Quiiiick–MUCH, Arf Eye, Arf Eye, Arf Eye . . . PICK IT UP PICKITUP! . . . Hahbout–TUH! . . . GET THE LEAD OUT!

For three weeks my days and nightmares were haunted by the foreign tongue of air force drill. And by thoughts of Brasso. In the hours before bedtime, the air in the Horse Palace reeked with Brasso's sharp tang. Shining our shoes and brass was a solid half-hour's work. We dared not leave it until morning for, if time ran out, even God could not protect the airman who went on parade with dirty brass.

I went to bed with brass in my head. It was still there when I awoke. The war raged on in Russia, Europe, and the Pacific, but I was a prisoner of brass. We learned the Brasso two-step: slip the metal button-stick, shaped like a long skinny U, under each button to protect the fabric; daub on the murky fluid; and rub, hard. Four buttons down the tunic front, two on the breast pockets, two on the cap plus the cap badge–solid brass with a garland of leaves embracing the letters *RCAF* and topped with a crown. And a tunic belt buckle. And *eight* buttons on the great-coat, airman-for-the-use-of. Rub, rub, rub . . .

New brass, coated with heavy air force–issue yellow varnish, was a heartbreaker. The *Pocket Guide for Trainees* told us to wet the new buttons with a good polish and "burn with match or lighter." For idiots, it added, "Be careful not to burn your uniform." Shrewder men bought sets of buttons ready buffed to a soft gleam, from equally shrewd airmen on the permanent staff, and lived Manning lives of ease and contentment. Naturally, I was too dumb and conscientious to do it in any but the hard way.

At six A.M. the lights blazed on to the ritual cry: "Wakey wakey wakey! Let go of yer cocks and grab yer socks!" We stepped onto the cement floor, as cold and slick as the Columbia Ice Field. We sprinted to stake out a sink. (For me, the endless gush of hot water was a treat after nineteen years of drawing water from the well and heating it in a basin on a coal stove.) We darted in and out of showers. We sat in stolid rows on the exposed toilets, gazing out with empty eyes. We gave our boots and buttons a last lick-and-a-promise. The four Ss—shit, shave, shine, and shampoo—were now complete. Six-forty-five and running hard.

We made our beds neatly, in constant dread of a snap inspection: one gray blanket taut on top, its bottom corners folded and tucked, second blanket primly folded at the foot with its stripe showing an even line. Everything else was stowed in the kit bag at the foot of the bunk. At home my mother made the beds. *Welcome to the real world, acey-deucy!*

By seven, into the noisy mess hall, heavy with morning smells. Two hard-boiled eggs rolled like grenades on my plate with two slabs of cooling toast, a slice or two of brittle bacon, and sticky jam from tins on the long tables. Our meals, it was said, were heavily laced with saltpeter to quell our libidos. Otherwise, the air force reasoned, hundreds of sex-crazed men confined to barracks might run amok, raping and pillaging the civilian secretaries and WDs. The truth was, most of us were too bone weary to have any leftover sex drive.

For our twenty-one days in Training Wing we worked six days a week, 7½ hours a day. Two hours of every day were spent on P.T. and games, three more on drill, and the rest in lectures: on drill, promotion, security, deportment, *esprit de corps*, pay and allowances, duties of sentries, and air force law.

P.T. back in Standon School had been casual and undemanding, conducted by soft pliant women teachers who never wore slacks or touched their toes. Here, our instructors were lean mean sadists with hard muscles. There were knee bends, arm stretches, runnings on the spot, jumps, bends. Pushups that I could barely do, my skinny frame pitiful in T-shirt and gym shorts as I tried to lift it on trembling arms. Pain in the feet, back, legs, the whole body screaming.

Then we scrabbled onto the parade square, yawning, wary, and sullen except for Sam Glassford. He marched into drill with the same ebullience he brought to everything else. His shoes and brass were always gleaming. He never sucked up to the NCOs but didn't mind volunteering when a job needed doing. Strangely, we didn't resent him for it.

"FALL IN!" We hurried like lemmings into three ranks.

"TEN-*SHUN*!" The NCOs hammered this ritual into our brains. It was all in the *Manual of RCAF Drill and Ceremonial*: Arms smartly to the sides, left foot brought against the right with a downward slam. Heels together and in line. Toes out at 45 degrees. Body ramrod straight, head erect, eyes straight ahead. Weight evenly distributed on both feet, shoulders drawn down and back "without straining or stiffening, arms hanging as straight as natural bend allows." Wrists straight, backs of hands outward, fingers bent inward at both joints, thumbs placed at the side of the forefingers at the middle joint; touching trousers lightly at side with thumbs immediately behind the seam of the trousers. *All this just to stand up?*

"RIGHT DRESS!" We thrust an outstretched right arm onto the shoulder of the man beside us and—*shuffle-shuffle-shuffle*—evened out the distance between ranks.

Then inspection. What would that son of a bitch sergeant find wrong this time? A streak of tarnish on the cap badge? A thicket of unshaven whiskers? A shadow of unkempt neck hair?

They knew exactly what they were looking for. Clean clothes. Boots and brass shining. Face shaved, hair cut. Wedge cap precisely placed with its lower button in the center of the forehead and cap pulled to the right so the front edge was one inch above the center of the right eyebrow. Collar clean and held in place by RCAF-issue collar pin. Buttons sewn on with the crown uppermost and the eagle flying horizontally (as any sensible eagle would). Pockets buttoned and not bulging.

And if we failed inspection? "CORPORAL, TAKE THAT MAN'S NAME AND NUMBER!" Usually it meant nothing worse than a joe-job but to me, earnest and obedient, the threat bespoke the dreaded digger, or maybe a firing squad at dawn.

"Stand at . . . *EASE*." Arms behind back, left foot twelve inches smartly to the left. Stand at ease was a misnomer; there was nothing easy about it. No movement was permitted. You could not scratch an itchy nose or buttock until the corporal cried "STAND EASY!" and "YOU MAY SMOKE IF YOU WISH." The ways of the air force were wondrous indeed.

Then: "AWRIGHT YOU MEN . . ." It always began that way, just as we were comfortably standing easy—the little ritual lecture, the mandatory reaming out to remind us the air force was boss. ". . . YOU ARE THE SLOPPIEST SCRUFFIEST SORRIEST LOOKIN' BUNCHA ERKS I'VE EVER SEEN BUT I'M GONNA MAKE AIRMEN OUTA YOU, SO YOU BETTER SMARTEN UP. . . ."

There *was* some rhyme and reason to it all, in the mind of the anonymous desk pilot who wrote the rules in the *Manual:*

> From the time a recruit enters the RCAF he is taught to take a pride in himself and his appearance, to acquire self discipline and self respect, to keep himself fit and to learn to cooperate with his fellows. From this beginning, esprit de corps is built up. . . .

Our flight commander was Sergeant J. Price, tall and angular, a decent man but sorely tried. His was not an easy lot. Every six weeks or so, a fresh batch of flotsam and jetsam from civilian life was thrown up on the beach of Sergeant Price's life. Little wonder that his gaunt face with its small neat mustache was set in an expression of permanent gloom.

On his first morning with Flight 197—trying to teach us such essentials as coming on parade not looking like bums and calling him "Sergeant" instead of "Sir"—he paused, breathing fire, in front of a roly-poly airman from North Winnipeg.

The recruit was maybe thirty, ancient by my standards, with the don't-give-a-damn air of a Depression survivor. He was the most frugal man I've ever known. My mother—herself a Depression-era virtuoso who made rags into rugs and used slop water to nourish her flower beds—would have been proud to have him for a son. When shaving he daubed his face with one small dollop of lather, scraped it off with the whiskers, then re-used the mess over and over. It was he who showed me that you could, theoretically, prolong a razor blade by honing it on the inside of a glass. It gave me some of the bloodiest, most agonizing shaves of my life. On this day he hadn't even done that.

"DID YOU SHAVE THIS MORNING, AIRMAN?" cried Sergeant Price in his voice of doom.

"No."

"NO, WHAT?" thundered Price. (Would these bastards *ever* learn to call him "Sergeant"?)

"No razor," said the man from North Winnipeg.

For this kind of aggravation, Price was paid $2.95 a day, maximum.

Corporal Collins, Tonto to the sergeant's Lone Ranger, played the role of beastly NCO with consummate skill. No doubt, somewhere, there was a mother who loved him. According to a fawning column in the camp paper, *The Airman's Post,* "our handsome corporal is popular with the boys after hours." Maybe with some boys but not with me. Maybe the NCO teams had prearranged scripts—good cop–bad cop—to keep us forever off balance. Be that as it might, the corporal habitually eyed us with the profound disgust of a man who has just stepped in dog shit. He spared no insult, no epithet, as Training Wing methodically began to take us apart, rid us of our nasty civilian ideas about individualism, and rebuild us into good marching machines. We hated him cordially in return. It was no fun for me, having the same name.

From dawn until dusk Price and Collins, and assorted other two-stripers and three-stripers, were ever on our backs. Long after the war, Fred McGuinness, a Brandon newspaperman active in civic projects, accepted a donation from a large Winnipeg company. It was to help Brandon build a center to replace the old Arena and Winter Fair complex.

"Come and see what we're doing with the money," McGuinness urged the donor.

"Never!" said the Winnipegger, a World War II veteran.

"Why not?"

"After what No. 2 Manning Depot did to me I don't want to *ever* set foot in that city again!"

Most of us left with similar, if less passionate, memories. The pragmatists among us made the best of it. At home, I'd been taught to respect my elders, speak only when spoken to, and always obey the Mounties (the only police around). My father paid his taxes when thousands did not. My mother endured misery with such stoicism that I half believed she enjoyed it. So, at Manning, did I.

Anyway, the air force had us, as the saying went, by the short hairs. We were in for the duration, which could be a very long time. In 1943 the Allied invasion of Europe was still a distant dream. Presumably, some appalling act could get you a dishonorable discharge, but few men considered that as a way out. We were firmly patriotic. Not long before, a senior officer had delivered a ringing message to all ranks, via *The Airman's Post.* It went in part:

Those German Beasts would hang their heads in shame—no, they have no shame—so they would ask for peace, if they could see the splendid type of determined manhood passing through No. 2 Manning Depot. Yes, the same fine fellows who are going to help crush for ever the evil spirit with which all dictators are inspired. We have a hard fight ahead, but with God's help there is no doubt as to who shall win the final battle.

We were not embarrassed by such rhetoric. We wanted to have the right stuff. Lead-swingers and dog-fuggers in our midst were not admired.

Having learned to stand, we were ready to walk. "QUIIIICK MARCH!" Head and body at attention, arms straight, "swinging back as far as comfortably possible and forward to waist level." Quick-march was a normal pace, distinguished from slow-march which was reserved for funerals or other glum occasions when the NCOs had nothing else to keep us busy. Hands closed but not clenched, thumbs pressed on forefingers and always to the front. "PICK UP THOSE FEET!"

Some men did not know how to swing the opposite arm in unison with the leading leg when they marched. A misfit who swung his left arm and left foot forward at the same time was always getting stepped on by the rabble behind him. It was always good for a screech from the corporal and a chuckle from the rest of us, on days when laughs were scarce.

"SQUAAAD . . . HALT!" The first word of every command was drawn out, to alert us for the action word. This one was delivered on the right foot and executed two beats later (*one-two-slam-the-foot*, we counted in our heads). Until finally, one triumphant morning, after hours of NCO shrieks of "AS YOU WERE!" (meaning, approximately, "go back and start over, you dummies!"), after infinite numbers of halts with a machine gun sputter of out-of-step boots, it actually *worked!* One-two-slam—thirty-eight men stopped with one resounding crack of ponderous feet, and I felt a little thrill of exultation.

We learned to turn right, turn left, turn about, without losing step or trampling one another to death. We mastered the change-step—a curious little hop-skip, a heavy-footed ballet. We "marked time"—marching on the spot, a useful maneuver if we were in imminent danger of running over a gaggle of old ladies on the street. We learned the "Eyes Right (or Left)," officially for use when passing an officer: the NCO snapped a salute, the rest of us gave him the eye, *en masse*. But sometimes on Brandon's streets when we were marching well and the NCO, in a generous mood, felt we deserved a treat, we gave Eyes Right to the nearest pretty girl, leaving her pink with confusion and secret pride.

We marched miles and miles in boots heavy as cement blocks. I was a stout walker. On the farm I'd hiked long distances fetching cattle, stooking grain, or just prowling the fields for pleasure. In high school I rode a bicycle eleven miles each day, uphill and down, usually into a stiff wind. But Manning's route marches were a challenge even for me, because the stiff unwieldy boots soon cut a raw wound in my left instep. I was too scared and proud to go on sick parade—*what if they accused me of fuggin' the dog?* Stoically, a true son of my mother, I limped grimly through drills and marches with pads of my own devising over the cut. Eventually it healed into a scar that lasted for years.

In time I came to enjoy the rhythm of drill. Maybe it was an echo of childhood, when I coaxed my father to give me marching orders in his military voice. Naturally, I admitted to none of this in the torrent of foul-mouthed bitching when we lounged around the Horse Palace at night.

Like any normal boy, I had heard dirty jokes and synonyms for sexual organs at school. I modestly held up my end in practice swearing behind the boys' privy at recess in Standon School. Now I realized I'd been playing in the minors. Here I was with professional scatologists: hard-bitten miners from Kirkland Lake, hard-luck guys from Winnipeg, and smart-asses from Toronto. I learned there were six or eight nicknames each for the male and female genitals, maybe more on a good day. And, although I was slow to join in, I laughed as hard as the next man. It was liberation from a puritanical upbringing. There was no one here to say "Shhh!"

For sheer creative cussing, we never measured up to our disciplinarians. One night after a grueling day on the parade square we lay flopped on our bunks, wondering whether we'd live until dawn, or wanted to. Suddenly Corporal Collins stalked among us. This meant trouble. Normally the NCOs were as glad to be rid of us as we were of them. He strode directly to my bed. My guts turned to jelly. But his wrath was aimed at a big strapping boy with a handsome saucy face, leaning indolently on his elbow in the bunk above me. Whatever his sin, from earlier that day, it was something Corporal Collins knew but couldn't prove. The corporal paused, for theatrical effect, and looked for a way to bait him. He noticed my bunkmate was munching a wad of Spearmint.

"There's only two kinds of people that chew gum," cried Corporal Collins, in a voice audible throughout Brandon. "Telephone operators and cocksuckers! And I know you're not a telephone operator!"

The big kid was no fool. One intemperate reply and he'd have been cleaning toilets with a toothbrush or quick-marching to the digger. Shrewdly he stayed silent, grinning insolently and snapping his gum. With a few more well-chosen words, Corporal Collins raged impotent into the night. . . .

We put on masks and stumbled through a blockhouse full of mustard gas, to be ready should the Nazis ever chase us through a blockhouse full of mustard gas. We began to sing on route marches, in step with the cadence, a sign we were becoming sure of ourselves or even—as the perennial gagline went—were "happy in the service." Often we sang the servicemen's anthem:

> Bless 'em all, bless 'em all
> The long and the short and the tall
> Bless all the sergeants and WO1s
> Bless all the corporals and their bastard sons . . .

We moved into rifle drill and I liked it. Long ago, my father had shown me a few maneuvers with the .22 in our farmyard. Now, unwarlike though I was, the Mark IV Lee Enfield felt good. *The real war at last?*

"Order—AHMS!" Rifle butt on the ground, flat against your right leg, gripped on the barrel at or near the sling, held perpendicular close to the body.

"Slope AHMS!" A tricky maneuver. You tossed the rifle up, vertically, with the right hand and, if you were lucky, caught it near the sling with the left. You held it lightly, perpendicular, facing outward. *Did you ever drop your rifle, Daddy? No, my child, but some poor benighted erk, lacking in motor skills, always did, to the terrible derision of his mates and the NCOs.*

Then, on command, the second movement: getting the rifle up onto the shoulder, in a manner so exacting that it took the *Manual* 101 words to describe it.

Soon we could "Present Arms" by numbers. "SQUAD ONE": we slapped the right hand across the body to grip the butt.

"SQUAD TWO": rifle moved to a perpendicular position, left

27

hand placed ("smartly," if the *Manual* had its way) against the stock.

"SQUAD THREE": still moving "smartly," we lowered the wretched weapon in front of us. Simultaneously, if our brains and body were working together that day, we raised the right foot nine inches from the ground, slammed it down ("smartly," of course) and stood stock still, the rifle about two inches clear of each blue-clad body. A pretty sight on a sunny day, when each slap and click and stamp came with chorus line precision.

We fired thirty rounds of ammo from twenty-five yards and learned to fix and unfix bayonets without cutting off our vital parts. The serious skills of war — real shooting, thorough gas attack training, and extensive drill under fire — were totally neglected. We were just being programmed to move, when told. The German hordes would have made mincemeat of us in a standing fight but, as I moved robotlike through the daze of Training Wing, surviving Corporal Collins seemed more urgent than getting ready for Hitler.

At night after supper we rested our feet and attacked the hated brass. I stoked up on Oh Henry bars, Cokes, and five-cent hot dogs at the canteen. On Wednesday and Friday nights I binged on free movies in the arena; at home, the sixteen-mile trip to the Gravelbourg cinema had been a luxury enjoyed only three or four times a year.

Often I just loafed on my bunk, getting to know my growing circle of friends, shyly letting out snippets of myself, painfully learning the art of conversation. Sometimes I scribbled a letter home on free YMCA stationery in the rec room, to the background *click-clock* of ping-pong balls. I missed my family, but not desperately. All my energies were bent on getting through this intense experience. I wrote them mundane letters — a would-be writer who had not yet learned to bare himself on paper. Anyway, I didn't want my parents to worry.

When training ended we got a "72." (Short leaves were described by hours: "36," "48," "72.") Sam and I rented a cheap room in a Brandon hotel and then didn't know what to do with it. I was not yet into beer drinking, preferring to abuse my body with sugary soft drinks. Getting a girl was beyond comprehension.

Brandon was a nondescript farm city of seventeen thousand, perched on the rim of a wooded river valley. Apart from A. E. McKenzie, the largest seed company in the British Empire, and a few grain elevators along the railway tracks, its profile was only two or three storeys high. It was a comfortable, nonfrightening city for a farm boy, but it was also awash with uniforms from the nearby flying schools and army base, far more than the local girl population could absorb.

The locals unlocked their daughters to meet the demand. There was a "dance hostess" service, providing partners for the weekly "hops" around the military community. The girls, according to *The Airman's Post,* were "carefully selected, must be over 17 years of age and unmarried and are drawn from the ranks of nurses and teachers, debs and domestics, stenographers and clerks. The selectees are reminded that the dances are designed for the enjoyment of the boys in blue and khaki and must be regarded by the girls as part of their war work. . . ."

Air crew, handsome ground crew, and well-built soldiers got these handpicked delicacies. There were none left over for an AC2 with raging acne, ill-fitting uniform, and a 125-pound body—especially if this misfit couldn't dance. Well, I'd never had a girlfriend. A stoic could wait a little longer. The most exciting thing I did was go for long walks with Glassford along the Assiniboine River which, after all, was more water in one place than I'd ever seen in my life.

Then one day, miraculously, Manning was over.

"Wanta chip in to buy a few beers for the NCOs?" somebody said. I had a hunch the NCOs fostered that tradition themselves. But most of us pitched in a quarter or fifty cents, partly because we didn't have the nerve to resist (what if Corporal Collins returned to haunt us in some future posting?), partly because we felt no lasting resentment toward them. They were not nearly as tough as Canadian Army disciplinarians or the sadistic U.S. Marines. They had done what the air force asked of them: turned us from self-indulgent civilians into competent military fodder. No hard feelings.

In fact, I was proud at having slogged through it. *Not everybody could march all those miles with a gaping raw wound on his left foot.*

Here we are in a yellowing photograph, Flight 197, newly graduated and ready to move on to the next adventure. There is Sergeant Price, actually *smiling,* and no wonder. His ordeal is over—until the next flight. There I stand, fresh faced, half smiling, ears jutting from my shorn head, neck protruding from my ill-fitting collar.

But who are these other men, my brothers in arms and

misery for six weeks? How could we live that intense relationship and be near-forgotten now? There's Sam Glassford;
I'll never forget him. And Norm McParland. But this cocky
face beside me . . . Laurie Andrechek? And the tall handsome one with the cheeky grin . . . of course, he's the one
who was *not* a telephone operator. But what was his name?
That chubby older man whose uniform fits, whose shirt
looks even tight around the neck . . . yes, he's "no razor"
from North Winnipeg. Other names come back out of the
mists: Ole Inget from Nipigon, Schneider from Regina,
Moon from Portage la Prairie, Toews from Sudbury. Are they
here?

I do not know. They and most others are forgotten and
the Public Archives of Canada in its infinite wisdom will not
give out the list of Flight 197, forty years later. Because . . .
what? I might seek them out and sell them encyclopedias?

Better, maybe, that I *not* find them; that they stay there
in the photo of 1943, forever young, full of hopes and dreams
and apprehension.

We finished training in late October. Of me, Sergeant Price
reported "Assessment: Good; Bearing and Deportment: Good.
Completed rifle training." I took the mandatory fourteen-hour
first-aid course and got my St. John Ambulance badge, which
I gratefully sewed onto the barren wasteland of my sleeve—no
rank insignia, no trade badge, just the routine shoulder patch
with a white eagle on a black background.

After Training Wing, we became Disposal Wing, meaning joe-
jobs until the next posting. We watched new recruits arrive, lost
sheep in civvies, and we veterans of six weeks chortled, "You'll
be sorr-eee!"

The postings came through for the next phase: training for our
trades. Out of twelve possible sites from Edmundston, New
Brunswick, to Vancouver, I drew Moose Jaw, sixty miles from
Shamrock. It was perfect. I'd be able to get home on leave. I
dashed off a gleeful note to my parents.

One cool October night—the military always moved us at
night—we marched out of No. 2 Manning to the westbound train,
singing "The North Atlantic Squadron":

> Away, away with fife and drum,
> Here we come
> Full o' rum,

30

Lookin' for women who peddle their bum
In the North Atlantic squadron . . .

Until a sergeant growled the all-purpose "AWRIGHT, YOU MEN!" in deference to the slumbering burghers of Brandon. We subsided, chuckling, and piled into day coaches at the little station that had seemed so vast and alien a mere six weeks before.

We were heady with relief and pride and excitement. *"Per ardua ad astra"* read the official RCAF motto. "Through adversity to the stars." Well, we'd survived a little adversity. Bring on the stars!

We *were* feeling that *esprit de corps*. We were *air force* and what could be better than that in the autumn of '43?

Chapter Four

We did not, of course, go "Heigh ho, Heigh ho'ing" off to work each day like Disney dwarfs or Nelson Eddy Mounties. But we *did* sing often on route marches—it helped us forget the mindlessness of our task—and in barracks and wet canteens. It was a singing war, the last real singing war in history, and those were the glory days of boogie-woogie and the big bands. We servicemen and -women *made* the big bands, and the bands imprinted their melodies on us forever. To this day, the opening bars of Glenn Miller's "In the Mood" send prickles up my scalp. . . .

I am back in a 1940s drill hall, *any* drill hall, a hundred drill halls. I stand on the sidelines, a nondancer, miserable and elated by turns, watching a swirling sea of blue uniforms and skirts spinning out like saucers, the whole room twirling, cavorting in the fever of the jitterbug.

Every big and little band on two continents emulates Miller's arrangement. "In the Mood" is *the* dance tune of the war. Hear it now! The alto saxes sprint with the tenors and trumpets. The trombones sigh. The music softens, fades . . . is it over? No! A rap of drums, the chorus surges back again, and then *again*, spiraling, soaring in a last crescendo that drives the dancers mad!

There are other tunes, other memories. A Tommy Dorsey trombone glides into "I'll Be Seeing You"—and, yes, I hear Sinatra's voice echoing over the P.A. system in the hangars at Mont Joli bombing and gunnery school, between bulletins from the orderly room and the drumming of Fairey Battle motors. Les Brown's "Sentimental Journey"—I am looking across a Belfast dance hall at a girl named Constance with whom, moments later, I will fall hopelessly in love.

Dorsey's "Moonlight Serenade" flowing over a dance floor like molten honey, Hal McIntyre's alto sax throbbing into "I'm Making Believe," Vaughn Monroe with muscles in his larynx singing "There I've Said It Again," Miller tingling our spines and tugging at our feet with "A String of Pearls" . . . each is a key that unlocks the memories of forty years.

Music came naturally to me. At home there was never a day without it. In school every morning we earnestly implored God to Save Our Gracious King. In church we shouted out "Holy, Holy, Holy, Lord God Almighty . . ." At Christmas concerts my brother and I sang solos or duets (our specialty: "When It's Lamplighting Time in the Valley"). Often the whole family sang together before bedtime just for fun. Sometimes I strummed the guitar, wailing western songs in a bad imitation of Wilf Carter— "Come a ki-yi yippy-yippyay-yippyay . . ." while my parents and Larry listened with strained smiles.

Whether or not my fellow airmen shared these musical roots, we were all of the radio generation. We had grown up *listening* and singing along, not just *looking* and eating potato chips. Now, in the canteens, movies, and drill halls, our heroes and heroines were Harry James, his silvery trumpet soaring through "The Two O'Clock Jump"; the Andrews Sisters with their locked-in harmony racing through "Boogie-Woogie Bugler Boy"; the mellow Mills Brothers murmuring "You Always Hurt the One You Love."

There were other songs, the kind you never sang for Mother. They were dirty, funny, and as integral to service life as Brasso and saltpeter. The rollicking old Scottish song "Road to the Isles" gave us the melody for the equally stirring "Nellie, Put Yer Belly Close to Mine." To the tune of "My Bonnie Lies Over the Ocean" we sang

> My brother's a poor missionary
> He saves all the girlies from sin
> He'll save you a blonde for five dollars
> My God, how the money rolls in!
>
> Rolls in, rolls in,
> My God how the money rolls in, rolls in!
> Rolls in, rolls in,
> My God how the money rolls in!

We were no more foul of mouth or mind than today's average

fourteen-year-old. On the contrary, most of us at eighteen or nineteen were sexually ignorant and severely repressed. In my childhood, sex was—I felt sure—never practised before marriage. In my fairly typical home, my good and decent parents never discussed it with or in front of us. If it accidentally reared its ugly head in conversation, it was smothered with a warning "Shhh!"

Now we were breaking out. It was not only acceptable but *mandatory* to talk and brag about the once-forbidden fruits. Since most of us had nothing to brag about, the next best was to sing of what we barely understood: obliging whores (we called them hoo-ers), buggery, and other dark arts that I couldn't even pronounce.

On the frosty October morning when we tumbled gummy eyed into Moose Jaw after sitting up all night on CPR day coaches, we swung up Main Street treating early risers to a parody of the grand old march "Blaze Away":

> Oh, this is the day that we give away babies with
> half a pound of tea,
> If you know any ladies who want any babies just
> send them up to me . . .

The passersby stared us down with eyes as cold as a taxman's heart. They'd heard it all before. Airmen were no novelty in Moose Jaw. Three of the fifteen air training bases in Saskatchewan were within easy range of the city. And here, on Main between Caribou and Hochelaga, blue-uniformed bodies were in endless supply, 150 of them at a batch. This was the Douglas Block, a two-storey brick box, home of the War Emergency Training Program (WETP). The acronym was obvious and we gleefully embraced it: Wet-Pee.

There were no barracks, but the air force pointed us at approved rooming houses. Sam Glassford and I found a tiny upstairs bedroom in a dowdy two-storey white stucco house run by a motherly Mrs. Locke, on River Street East just a nudge and a wink from Moose Jaw's red-light district. It had a hip roof, and we were always cracking our heads on its slanting ceilings, but after the Horse Palace it was heaven.

It was Friday so we got a weekend pass. There was just time to catch the 10:30 A.M. local to Shamrock. For the next four hours the freight cars and single day coach would lurch and puff and buck and grumble through Caron, Old Wives, Courval, Coderre, and Trewdale until the CPR deposited me in Shamrock at 2:30. Plenty of time to savor the sweet excitement of going home.

"Home" was my anchor. Through the farm years our family

had been inseparable. All day my parents worked within sight or sound of each other, she at her chickens and kitchen and garden, he with the horses and cows and endless repairs of buildings, harness, fences, and machinery. Even in the fields he was never more than a hill or two out of sight. Indoors, he helped her dry dishes. Outdoors, she helped him milk cows.

We ate together, read together, went to town together. When my brother and I came home from school we raced to show our father our latest A's and he always praised us. When at age ten I discovered mortality and woke one night blubbering, "I'm going to *die* in sixty more years!", my mother comforted me and didn't laugh. Once she went to hospital in Vanguard, forty-five miles away, and our world turned upside down. Sometimes my father had to spend two nights in Regina at a veterans' medical board and was always so lonesome he phoned home at least once.

Now, although I had been away only six weeks, it seemed *so* long ago. Radical change had come to us all in those weeks. I had left from the farmhouse that my father built for my mother in 1920, the place where I was born, a place that had seemed as permanent as eternity. Now they were five miles north in a new little home on the edge of Shamrock. During the move our favorite dog had been killed by a car. I would see them in a totally new environment, and they would see me in air force blue.

The train snorted triumphantly into Shamrock station almost on time. I raced home to hug my mother. *Was her hair grayer than before?* My brother was still at school. I headed back toward town where my father managed Imperial Building Supplies. But he'd already locked up early and was trudging toward me, a distant figure on the railway tracks. *Was he more stooped than before?* He uttered a great roar, "Hiya, Brother!", an affectionate nickname of old, not as personal as "Son" but this was a delicate moment for us both as I strode toward him, uniformed, transformed from boy to man. Then we threw our arms around each other and it was all right.

The weekend fled through heaping chicken dinners, enormous breakfasts, and talk, talk, talk.

"Are they giving you enough to eat, Son?"

"Yeah, but they sure can't cook like you!"

"You look taller!"

"It's the drill. They kill you for not standing up straight. *You* know about that, eh Dad?"

He knew. He was beside himself with pride, curiosity, and a

35

smattering of envy but he never once mentioned his war, as other veterans might have. This was my day and he refused to steal it from me.

I told them everything and nothing. All the funny things and none of the pain. All about Sam and the man who re-used his shaving cream and the misfits who dropped their rifles on their toes. Nothing of that first bleak night or the dressings-down from the NCOs or the humiliating short-arms or Fuck the East.

I taught my brother the only clean air force song I knew — already at fifteen he played banjo and trumpet in a dance band — and soon we were harmonizing on

> There were rats, rats, big as alley cats in the
> stores, in the stores;
> There were rats, rats, big as alley cats, in the
> Quartermaster's stores . . .

My father grinned. *He* knew there were other songs.

They still had one foot in farming. Their little acreage supported two cows, a flock of chickens, and the mandatory half-acre garden. But my mother with her bottomless energy was also a pillar of the village church and the Women's Auxiliary.

On Saturday my father walked me to the post office and McCrary's Corner Store to show me off. To my secret disappointment, no one made a fuss. I was only lowly ground crew, and I'd been gone only six weeks *(but couldn't they see how far I'd soared in that time?)*.

At least Mister Adams, the postmaster, warm and gracious as usual, complimented me on my uniform. Later he came to take a family group photograph and a single of me which, there being no color film in those days, he hand tinted as a gift for my parents. I looked out at the camera, shy, thin, tentative yet perceptibly older than the boy of six weeks before. It would remain framed on my mother's bureau for the rest of the war.

Suddenly it was Sunday night and I was back on River Street East with a boxful of homemade cookies, glad to have been home but ready to get on with the adventure. We started training the next morning.

In Moose Jaw that October 25, 1943, milk was selling at ten cents a quart, T-bone steak at thirty-seven cents a pound, and fancy McIntosh apples at twenty-seven cents for three pounds. Ronald Colman was starring in *Lost Horizon* at the Orpheum and the Royal featured Bogart and Ingrid Bergman in *Casablanca*.

36

The tide had turned in the Russian-Nazi war. The Moose Jaw *Times-Herald* shrieked

GREAT POWER CITIES OF DNIEPER ARE TAKEN NAZI DISASTER MOUNTS AS REDS UNCHECKED

Were we trainees already redundant? Not yet. The RCAF still wanted men. Its recruiting ad showed a trim pilot with flawless skin (naturally, they never pictured an erk with pimples) demanding "What's holding *you* back, brother?" Nothing was holding *us* back! We were ready to learn to fix airplanes.

By autumn 1943 the WETP was turning out air force technicians in sixteen cities. Our Douglas Block trained in airframe, aero engine, and wireless. Working in part on the stripped-down bodies of Gypsy Moths and Tiger Moths, each airframe class of thirty or forty—ours was Flight 92—took six consecutive courses over eighteen weeks. After each three-week stint we had an oral and written exam. In the real war, these little wood and fabric aircraft were already obsolete, so most of what I learned in Moose Jaw would be useless. Luckily I didn't know it then, and plunged into Wet-Pee with enthusiasm.

We cut, planed, chiseled, and sanded aircraft ribs and spars. I loved the scent of fresh sawdust and the shapes (however plain) emerging like sculpture from slabs of wood. We patched fabric aircraft wings and bodies with "dope," a potent, wondrous-smelling form of glue (the wonder being that it didn't turn us all into addicts). In deafening chorus we shaped and pounded sheet metal, and welded and soldered joints with a sizzle and hiss. We each made a handsome useless tin funnel. We learned the rigging of an aircraft: the angles and workings of rudders and ailerons and trim tabs. I was less skilled than the best of us but less clumsy than the worst of us. And I was helping beat Hitler.

Best of all, we learned how an airplane flies. There was something magical and cerebral about it compared with all the hammering, cutting, and drilling. It touched the creative core of me. Forty years later I can still sketch an airfoil: in simplest terms, a cross section of a wing or tailplane—rather like a horizontal teardrop, with a rounded front, a tapering tail, a curved top, and a flattened underside. I can explain how, given forward thrust from a motor, an airfoil will fly: the onrushing air flows smoothly over its upper side, clinging to its streamlined contour, but swirls turbulently beneath the flat underside. That turbulence creates "lift."

It was the only air force course where I ever earned high marks. In subsequent months and years, theory-of-flight examiners would say to me admiringly, "You really *like* this, don't you!" I did, and in time might even have instructed in it. No one ever thought of that. Wars are great wasters of the living as well as the dead.

We fell into a comfortable routine. Sam and I shared a front room with a sagging double bed. He rose at 6:30 each black and frigid morning. His first act was to massage his hands and chest vigorously to get the blood flowing, whatever the weather.

"Up and at 'em, Lad!" he'd cry enthusiastically. "It's daylight in the swamp!"

We jockeyed with our fellow roomers for a turn at the toilet and sink (years later, none of us could remember using the bathtub). Eldon Fairburn was tall and straight backed with wavy hair and an air of *savoir faire* surprising in a kid from Delisle, Saskatchewan. Reg Starks from Colonsay was a shy farmer like me, two years older, with a serious clean-cut profile and a measured deliberate way of speaking. I came to know them better than the two Easterners—Norm Haddon, dark, pale, and taciturn, and big bespectacled "Westy" Westendorp—who were six weeks ahead of us in the course.

Breakfast was swift, subdued, and uninteresting. Then, swathed in blue mufflers, greatcoat collars turned up, and—unless the weather threatened to snap our ears like icicles—wearing our stylish wedge caps rather than the warm, sensible, dumb-looking, bowl-shaped Piss Pots, we swung down River Street, heavy boots ringing in the frosty dawn. Up First Street, down Cordova past the Grant Hall Hotel, right turn down Main and into Wet-Pee in ten minutes.

Classes began at eight and Sam always got me there on time. We worked until 5 P.M. (noon on Saturdays) with an hour for lunch. Sometimes we broke for a route march, pausing at small grocery stores on remote streets along the way to feed our acne with soft drinks and jam tarts and fruit pies and icing'd pastries. No doubt the NCOs were getting sticky bun kickbacks for laying this bonanza at the storekeepers' feet.

It was a wonderful unmilitary winter. Rooming at Mrs. Locke's felt more like coming home from a civilian job. Although we were under the watchful eye of a handful of RCAF personnel, the courses were given by civilian instructors, most of them friendly

38

older men. The work was not too demanding. I began to relax and have fun.

Food and the opposite sex were foremost on our minds. Food was easier for most of us to find. In our very midst at Wet-Pee, Johnstone Dairies had a snack bar called the Country Club, a glutton's paradise of white and chocolate milk, ice cream, shakes, soggy toast, jam, sandwiches, coffee, and chocolate bars. On midmorning and afternoon breaks we milled outside taking our cholesterol fix, jostling, joking, posing with feigned nonchalance for every passing girl and whistling at the prettiest ones.

We always wore hats outdoors; our pompous, nasty-tempered little warrant officer first class saw to that. Sam, Reg, and Norm wore their hair close clipped even though the rules were less stringent here. Eldon and I stroked and Brylcreemed and Vitalised ours into a cockscomb pluming proudly from the left side of the wedge cap. We all had our reasons. Sam had a wife, Edna, and two kids in New Liskeard and, officially, was not looking at girls. Reg, as decent and true a man as I've ever met, could think of no one but Anne, his fiancee at home. Eldon and I were on the open market.

For all our preening and posturing, our pleasures were mostly simple. Once Reg brought his father's car from home and promptly clipped off a Moose Jaw fire hydrant. It really made our day. Often we hung around the boarding house, flopped on one another's beds, yarning, griping about the air force, and, as we came to trust one another, revealing our pasts and hopeful futures.

Reg's dream was marriage and a farm of his own. Sam had a job waiting at Northern Hydro when the war ended. Eldon and I were free as the breeze. I didn't dwell on my writing plans. In these macho surroundings it would have seemed puzzling and effete. But I had signed up for a correspondence course on the installment plan from the Newspaper Institute of America (slogan: "How Do You Know You Can't Write?"). Its battered manual would travel in the bottom of my kit bag for the rest of the war. Whenever I could steal a quiet hour in a library or Canadian Legion, Salvation Army or YMCA writing room I'd mail off an assignment. Eventually a glowing appraisal came back from anonymous experts in New York. Part of me suspected that the critiques would never be harsh as long as I kept up the payments. The rest of me found the praise too seductive to resist.

I couldn't hide this from Sam—we practically lived inside each other's pockets – but he didn't laugh. At the time I chalked it up to his kindness but forty years later I learned that *he'd* had literary yearnings, for writing poetry, although strictly as a hobby. He kept his secret from all of us. He was a popular man-among-men and poetry would have ruined his image.

In Moose Jaw, a wonderfully compact city of 22,500, you could walk almost anywhere in a half-hour. It suited our style and our pocketbooks. We were mere steps from the cinemas, dance halls, and Crescent Park, a little green gem with trees (not common in southern Saskatchewan), benches, a footbridge and stream in the city's heart. Our legs were hardened like pig iron from route marches and we walked miles up and down streets with one another. If one man fell out of step he automatically did the half-shuffle CHANGE-STEP to get back in. Manning had programmed us better than we realized.

Automatically, too, we looked for girls to whistle at or – dared we hope? – *date*. Failing to find any, we studied the Moose Jaw *Times-Herald* and went to movies with one another. This was the fare offered on December 18, 1943.

> At the Capitol: *Behind the Rising Sun.* The shocking truth about the Sons of Heaven! They force their daughters into gilded Geisha palaces! They manhandle captive women! They torture prisoners! SEE IT ALL!

And we ate. The boarding house meals were barely adequate. Downtown Moose Jaw was dotted with eateries all called "cafe" – the Savoy, National, New Paris, New World, Modern, Princess, Exchange, Ambassador. Many were operated by genial Chinese who served filling but unimaginative occidental meals – mashed potatoes, sausage, black-fried eggs – the like of which they didn't dream of eating themselves. We haunted these places, gulping Cokes made from a potent soda fountain syrup, gobbling slabs of raisin and apple pie *à la mode*, eroding our teeth and appeasing the growling monsters that lived in our stomachs. My bony frame began to fill out but my skin looked like London after the blitz.

> A Pimple Covered Face Kills Many a Romance. Burdock Blood Bitters helps to cleanse the blood and with the blood cleansed the complexion should clear up.

Should clear up? I wanted guarantees. I used a harsh brown ointment that looked worse than acne. Sometimes it worked but my inferior skin and body did nothing for my self-confidence.

Most airmen of my acquaintance were chronically horny. The incessant talk of sex was an aphrodisiac. Yet in terms of male-female relationships I was severely retarded. I had never seen a naked woman, except in the *National Geographic*. I had never even seen a siren in a bathing suit; there were no swimming pools around home, and only one dribbling creek about twenty miles east. In grade eleven I almost swooned each time Bertie Lynn, an uncommonly pretty grade twelve, rolled her stockings above her knees at her desk after recess. Donny Robinson, Gordon McNeill, and I relished this twice-daily flash of tender thigh from our vantage point in the back row, praying that she would never buy a garter belt.

I arrived in the RCAF still savoring my only kiss, given out the night before I left home—dryly but charitably, like Maritimes codfish—by a girl I'd mooned over for three fruitless years. I had never been on a date.

Now it was time to begin. Sam egged me on. Marjorie Locke, the landlady's daughter, was a striking brunette with dark eyes and crimson lips. One day I bit the bullet and invited her to a movie. She accepted. *Good grief, now what?* I shaved with a new Minora blade; damn the expense. (Its makers promised "swell shaves" at four blades for ten cents.)

We had a choice of films. Roy Rogers and Trigger were at the Royal in *Song of Texas*. The Capitol offered *So Proudly We Hail* with Claudette Colbert, Paulette Goddard, and Veronica Lake. ("They're our women at the Fighting Front! Side by side in battle with the men they love!") We settled for Bing Crosby in *Pennies from Heaven* at the Orpheum.

It went well enough and ended with a couple of warm and professional (on her part) smooches at the foot of her mother's stairs. But I detected gentle amusement in her eyes. Soon she was going steady with Eldon. Although jilted, I bore him no grudge. He was handsome and self-assured and had muscles and clear skin. Why wouldn't a girl like him best?

Fun in Moose Jaw, as in most cities during the war, meant dancing. Every Thursday night Walter Budd and His Blossoms, heavy on the strings, held forth at the Oddfellows Hall; other nights it was the Rhythm Kings. The YMCA threw free dances every Saturday night. The Legion Hall, the New Empire Hall, and the Armouries held dances and jitterbug contests. The grandest of all was Temple Gardens ("Cal Temple, Mgr.") just around the corner from the Grant Hall Hotel: twenty-five cents before 9 P.M., thirty-five cents after, but even Eldon was too awed to go there.

My problem was basic: I couldn't dance. My parents were good dancers. There was music and rhythm locked somewhere deep inside me. But teenage shyness and awkwardness had conspired to build an enormous mental and physical block. On the farm I had failed to learn by correspondence, with portable paper footprints that I followed earnestly around the living room like an anthropologist tracking Bigfoot. My mother tried to teach me but my limbs froze up. Schoolhouse dances were ordeals; mostly I skulked behind the furnace.

It had to change. Air force life as a nondancer was not worth living. Under "Dancing Academies" in the yellow pages was a single listing: the Wynjoy Studio of Dancing at 318 Main North. I walked in tentatively one evening. It was a plain narrow room with two or three sturdy young women diligently chewing gum and waiting for prospects. They cranked up "Juke Box Saturday Night" on the record player, a "peppy number" in the parlance of the day. One of them seized me in an iron grip and galloped me up and down the hall.

"Maybe something slower," she suggested afterward, as we fell back panting. We stepped out, or more accurately I stepped on her, to Glenn Miller's "Serenade in Blue." After that we both knew it was a lost cause. I paid my money and slunk defeated into the night.

Finally, Sam goaded me into a blind date and I met a girl who tolerated my indifferent looks and lack of social skills. Mae Jean, from a small prairie town, had a sense of humor and no illusions of beauty. We usually double-dated with her pal Christine and some other stray airman—movies, Coke and pie, long walks, and increasingly fervent necking, her glasses freezing my nose in the bitter chill of a winter night.

Nothing else happened, although not for lack of interest on her part. One night she tossed me a riddle.

"What's the fruit that never ripens?"

"I dunno. I give up."

"A green pear."

I laughed weakly. We *were* a green pair; steeped in the *theory* of sex though I now was, I was definitely weak on the *practical* side.

I was still so uneasy with girls—a psychiatrist would have had a field day with me—that I was embarrassed on dates to excuse myself to go to the john. By the end of an evening I would be prancing in agony, barely able to contain myself, praying for the last good night so I could spring into the nearest alley to relieve myself. It put a damper on romance.

We were approaching another wartime Christmas. The *Times-Herald* said there'd be no Christmas trees this year unless farmers hauled them to the cities themselves; all laborers were needed for the war effort. I did not feel deprived; throughout the Depression my family had managed nicely with an artificial tree that folded out like an umbrella. Its make-believe needles and red cardboard berries looked authentic to my brother and me; we'd never seen the real thing.

In the city shops, toy planes and tanks were favorite gifts for small boys. Waterman sold "The Commando" ("The Pen on Active Service") for men and women overseas, $5.95 including excise tax. They even had blue and brown pens to match your uniform. Stanfield's, while not exactly pushing underwear for gifts, boasted, "Many of our gallant airmen are protected by Stanfield's Underwear against extreme cold at great heights." Smith Bros. Cough Drops, not to be outdone, advised:

CARELESS TALK MAY LOSE LIVES
Don't be careless about a cough

In Moose Jaw as in other cities, housewives had to plan their holiday shopping with care. Tea, coffee, sugar, butter, and preserves were rationed. So were beef, veal, pork, mutton, and lamb—from 1 to 2½ pounds per week, depending on the kind. Organ and processed meats were not rationed, which explained the preponderance of liver and bologna around the dinner table on River Street East.

Wet-Pee granted us a "72" over the Christmas weekend. On December 20 an ambulance rushed me to hospital at No. 32 Elementary Flying Training School outside of town, with gastroenteritis, the influenza that had already killed seventy Canadians that winter, and a temperature nearing 103. Sam phoned my parents, urging them not to worry, and the hearty assurance of his voice relieved them. They never met him, but came to regard him as a surrogate son.

Christmas Eve dawned gray and mild. Radio CHAB said Berlin was aflame from Allied raids and the featured program that night would be *The Christmas Carol*. I couldn't spend Christmas in this sterile place. Still burning with fever but faking good spirits, I begged my way out in time to catch a bus home. There they opened the living room davenport into a bed. On Christmas Day I sat propped among pillows, family around me, and feasted on chicken, mashed potatoes, and mountains of mince tarts.

On the twenty-seventh, I was still pale and shaky but due back on duty in a day. My father eagerly took charge. Here was something he could do. He knew how to handle the military—he thought. He phoned Wet-Pee to beg an extension of leave. We'd need medical proof that I was really ill, said the voice in Moose Jaw. Our nearest doctor was twenty miles away over impassable roads. My dad phoned the district nurse who, after hearing the symptoms, advised me to stay in bed. I returned to Wet-Pee six days late, sure that all was well. Sam looked at me oddly.

"Better go on sick parade first thing in the morning," he advised. "You're on the shit list!"

The medical officer, a cold-eyed Brit, pronounced me well (which, of course, I was by then), asked for the nonexistent letter from my doctor, looked down his patrician nose, and dismissed me with an icy, "As far as I am concerned, this man was absent without leave." AWOL! It meant the digger for sure!

A corporal marched me into the Orderly Room before the runty warrant officer. " 'TEN-SHUN!" He railed and jeered at me for ten minutes: "You think this air force is some kinda party where you stay home when you feel like it? . . . What's this little jerk-off place that doesn't have a doctor? . . . STAND AT ATTENTION! . . . whaddya have, a traveling midwife?" The corporal laughed obediently.

"I'm gonna . . . STAND UP STRAIGHT! . . . give you a break this time," he wound up. "I'm not gonna put you on charge . . . STRAIGHTEN THAT BACK! . . . but don't let me EVER see you in here again. You'll lose your next '48,' of course. DIS-MISSED!"

I slunk out, feeling lucky to be alive.

"It's all bullshit, Lad," Sam predicted. "You'll get your '48.' " He was right; it came through with all the rest, but I had believed the WO1 to the last moment and made no plans. He had his final revenge.

I was naively angry. They should have believed me; my father and I did not lie. And the warrant officer *did* lie. I went on being a dutiful airman—I couldn't do it any other way; my parents had rubbed it into my pores—but the first small crack of disillusionment had set in.

"Forget about it, Lad," Sam said philosophically. "They're all assholes! Ya know the old Latin motto? *No Illegitimus Carborundum!* Don't let the bastards grind ya down!"

The richest legacy of that Moose Jaw winter was my friendship with Reg, Eldon, and Sam. Starks, model of every virtue I'd been taught, simply made me glad there were still men like him around. Fairburn demonstrated the art of putting one's best foot forward; much later he confessed, to my amazement, that he was as unsure of himself and inexperienced with women as I that winter. And Sam, with the maturity of his twenty-eight years, was teaching me how to cope outside the safe cocoon of home and family. With them, I dared do things I'd never have done on my own.

Of course, nothing we did was very daring by later standards. A later generation grew up believing the world was theirs, if only it lasted. Ours knew the world would last forever but we were not at all sure we were worthy of it.

Chapter Five

Sometimes, to get a rise out of the Easterners, we Westerners sketched a crude map of Canada and superimposed on it a cruder cow. The bovine's head grazed on the prairie provinces, clearly stating that the whole nation fed and fattened on the West. Ontario drew milk from her teats (*ah, wasn't it the truth!*). Her rear end was poised over Quebec, implying that French Canada was always being dumped on, or was the ass end of Canada. Your interpretation depended on whether you were a Quebecer or a prairie redneck.

This always inspired profane debate, but on one point we all agreed: Ontario was the favored land. Now I knew for sure, as I first laid eyes on it during that last week of March 1944. We were headed for No. 5 Radar School in Clinton, a temporary stop en route to Technical Training School, St. Thomas, and our last twelve weeks of training. Past Winnipeg, our CPR train melted into a blur of evergreen, here and there a gleaming stand of birch, a woodland stream—sights wonderful and foreign to my prairie eyes. All day we rattled through this forest kingdom of northern Ontario, and this was only the *beginning*.

Friday, March 31, 1944, 6:15 A.M. We are entering Toronto, citadel of The East! I have had a love-hate affair with this place for years. From here comes one of my favorite radio shows, "The Happy Gang." Here the King and Queen, on their historic visit to Canada in 1939, spent days (not just a half-hour, as in Moose Jaw). From here, no doubt, came those shipments of castoff clothing for us prairie ragamuffins.

We roll through its miles of suburbs into immense Union Station, a travelers' cathedral. Marble floors and stairs, churchlike windows arching high, a ceiling vaulting eighty-

46

eight feet overhead, a vast rotunda echoing with glad hellos and tearful goodbyes. The rows of gates disgorge more people in a morning than the entire population of Moose Jaw.

"Big enough for you, Lad?" Sam says with an Easterner's grin. Eldon, Reg, and I gape in silence. Wouldn't you *know* Toronto would have marble!

We change for southwestern Ontario. Back home Saskatchewan is barely out of its annual deep-freeze. Here the land is smiling with spring: immaculate fields sprouting green; plump indolent cows; barns clad in sparkling fresh coats of red paint; thickets of trees with gnarled old trunks and tender bursting leaves. I can not tear my eyes from the window. It is a *Saturday Evening Post* cover come to life. It is exactly what I've suspected. Ontario has it all.

For two weeks, awaiting space at St. Thomas, the air force kept us at joe-jobs in Clinton. The serviceman's hoary joke, "I want three volunteers: you, you, and you!", was literal truth. For two weeks I washed dishes and set mess hall tables. *Was this why I joined the bloody air force?* At least I got plenty to eat. Then, bending under kit bags laden with everything we owned, we entrained one afternoon for St. Thomas, a mere hundred miles from Clinton. The trip took five hours.

"There were endless hours of wasting time," I grumbled in a letter home, sounding like an old veteran. "By now we know this outfit is famous for killing time."

I had phoned my parents before leaving for the East but, given only two days' notice, did not go home. In the five Moose Jaw months, a mere sixty miles away, I went home only twice and phoned only three or four times. It wasn't for lack of caring. But with no weekend train to Shamrock, getting there meant someone had to ferry me twenty miles to and from the mainline at Chaplin, an imposition in times of gasoline rationing. (Our own 1929 Chev was now inactive; my father never really trusted it.) Even a ten-minute long-distance call at seventy-one cents seemed a wild extravagance on $1.30-a-day pay. Depression penury was branded on my soul.

I made up for it with letters, an average of one a week, basic postage four cents, airmail seven cents. In those days the Canadian post office *worked.* One Monday morning I sent an airmail letter from St. Thomas that reached Shamrock—including the last four-hour leg by local train—the next afternoon.

I loved to send and receive mail: occasionally to my cousins, the Veseys, or Mister Adams back home, but mostly to my brother and parents. As I told them

April 15, 1944

It sure is nice to get a fat newsy letter every once in a while. Everybody crowds around at mail time and the poor cusses that don't get a letter for days at a time look pretty glum when their name isn't called out.

The very act of writing was a pleasure. I was getting the hang of service life but it was a life of physical and mechanical skills, with little for the mind. Letters were my refuge. Some of my happiest hours were spent in the blessed silence of a writing room or huddled on my bunk closing my mind to the incessant noise, scribbling on air force letterhead provided by the Canadian Legion, Knights of Columbus, YMCA, or Salvation Army.

Gradually my handwriting grew more assured. The letters, though not profound, were growing richer in detail and attempted humor. They found many things "grand," "dandy," or "lovely." This was not merely wide-eyed wonder. I wanted to assure my family that all was well. Increasingly I griped about military wrongheadedness, but that was a serviceman's right and duty. I carefully shielded my parents from such disturbing facts of life as drinking—I was now gingerly sampling beer—or girls. My letters never used an expletive stronger than "darn."

I pictured my envelopes with the blue *Per Ardua Ad Astra* crest and faraway postmarks tumbling out of Box 43 in Shamrock's tiny post office, along with Eaton's catalogue, the Regina *Leader-Post*, and the latest exhortation from the Liberal government urging the home folk to buy War Bonds, save sugar, or otherwise bend their backs to the war effort.

"So where's he at now?" the neighbors would ask, elbow to elbow with my father, casting sidelong glances at one another's mail.

"Down East," my dad would answer proudly. I'd see him reading the letter to my mother and Larry—he loved to read aloud—around the round oak dining table. Home looked warm and precious in those reveries. Sometimes—oh sacrilege!—it looked better from afar than when I was there. Being the center of attention by mail gave me the best of both worlds.

Their letters to me told all the important small events in their lives. My brother had an 86.2 average in his high school finals and, although still in his teens, was earning so much money playing trumpet and banjo with The Melody Knights that he'd bought a fifty-dollar War Bond. My mother's purebred chickens had passed the necessary tests once again. My father finally had a paid holiday from the niggardly Imperial Building Supplies. Important events to me, too, because this was home and sanity and order. It was permanence in a restless world. It was what we hoped we were preserving by going to war.

My letter to them of April 15 described our arrival at TTS the night before, lugging the infernal kit bags, lining up and waiting for bedding, lining up and waiting to be assigned to quarters, lining up and waiting for the mandatory medical. We were now almost blasé about the short-arm, exposing ourselves to the MO like practised flashers. At 10 P.M. we attacked a meal, our first since morning, and fell into bed before the 11:30 lights-out. At six the next morning, a Saturday, they roused us out for mess hall duty.

April 15, 1944

> That was a dirty deal but we got off after dinner. We were given a few lectures and a buck-toothed corporal laid down the law. At last, this afternoon, we got time to unpack.
>
> This place is huge. It was originally intended for a nut-house or, to be more exact, a sanitarium. . . . Once we find our way around we can get to know the place but right now a guy doesn't dare go off the beaten track or he might be lost for weeks. They say the place is full of skeletons of lost airmen, but they all turn up for pay parade. . . .

My description, although graceless, was accurate: we *were* in a former mental hospital—our second in six months if you counted Manning Depot's early history. The windows were still barred, inspiring the clowns among us to cling to them, screaming hysterically, "LEMME OUT, LEMME OUT!" The $7 million hospital had been turned over to National Defence for the duration. By the time of our arrival it had trained 35,000 trades personnel; it would train another 10,000 before war's end.

It was the biggest establishment in the entire British Commonwealth Air Training Plan. It made the Horse Palace look like a stable. On that April day it held 3,600 people: military and civilian staff plus 2,136 trainees. Its twenty-five handsome limestone buildings—row upon row, up to three storeys high—sprawled amid 487 acres of grounds. It took ten minutes just to walk along the frontage and hours to traverse the fifteen to eighteen miles of corridors and connecting underground tunnels. The tunnels, built to contain wandering patients, now served to confuse wandering airmen. So did the 2,500 doors.

Yet once we solved the maze, TTS was not forbidding. There was no excuse for boredom, thanks to the YMCA and Canadian Legion. For jocks, there were softball, hardball, swimming, you name it. For extroverts there were public speaking classes, drama club, and dances. For those with an artistic bent there were glee club, camera club, and art club (where the favorite question "Do we get nude models?" got a resounding "No!"). For me there were the station library with four thousand books, a writing room, movies nearly every night, and occasional variety concerts. In June, for instance, I saw Disney Studios' Clarence Nash, the voice of Donald Duck. To a city sophisticate, the spectacle of a grown man on stage talking like a duck must have seemed rather small beer. To me, it was Hollywood leaping off the screen of the Gravelbourg movie house before my wondering eyes.

We bought souvenir booklets about TTS, which boasted that, in the kitchen, 15,000 doughnuts were made at a batch and "a large herd of cattle is disposed of every day." The two 500-man dining halls couldn't handle us all at one sitting, so we ate in shifts. The cooks were divided into teams of specialists: roast cooks, soup cooks, bakers. The food was never as bad as we claimed but bitching about it was a knee-jerk reaction in which I cheerfully shared.

April 21, 1944

> The free show tonight is *Action in the North Atlantic* starring Humphrey Bogart. Probably something that'll make your blood curdle. After the cold salad we had for supper nothing more could make my blood curdle. . . .

Our quarters were austere but elegant: tile walls, chrome showers, terrazzo floors. We slept in six three-storey "wings" at the rear of the complex, each divided into twelve-man bays. Reg, Eldon, Sam, McParland, and I stuck together. Close by were Cooper, Sisterson, Inget, Kuh-nurled Kuh-nob, and a new friend Chuck Howard, a robust boy with ruddy cheeks. "We all have a lot of fun together and that was all that kept the morale up this far," I wrote home after a week in TTS.

But we soon learned the ropes. Our Moose Jaw roommates, Haddon and Westendorp, posted here ahead of us, filled us with TTS wisdom—the "straight gen" (accurate information). The opposite was "duff gen," in the prevailing slang, which had filtered into Canada from England's Royal Air Force. We eagerly adopted all these new buzzwords. We fancied they impressed fathers, small brothers, Army trainees, and other underprivileged folk.

On the shift system, Norm and Westy explained, we'd rise one week at 7 A.M. and go to bed at 11:30 P.M. (0700 hours and 2330 hours in military terms); the alternate week, 6 A.M. and 10:30 P.M. Sometimes we'd be hauled out to attend the daily flag-raising ritual at 7:45, complete with bugler.

We would work six days a week, with Saturday afternoon spent marching. There'd be one "36" and one "48" per month, and one 2 A.M. pass on the other weekends. Sunday morning church parade was mandatory but the rest of the day was free.

"I'm getting along fine," my first letter ended, "and I'm anxious to get into the stuff again after that darned dish washing."

The "stuff" began on Monday when, clad in coveralls and lumped into Entry 205, we began a thorough review and enhancement of our Wet-Pee training. Hour after hour, our numb buttocks anchored to wooden benches in the crafts shops, we labored over our lessons. We watched movies about hydraulics, the mystifying (to me) system of fluid pumped from reservoirs to operate aircraft brakes, shock-absorbing legs, and other controls. I learned that the hydraulic legs on, say, a Fairey Battle bomber and a Harvard trainer were different, and I'd better care.

April 21, 1944

> It's so dull and stuffy in the shops, when the weather is so nice outside. . . . You can learn a lot from the movies but in a dark warm room it's about all a guy can do to keep awake. . . .

I didn't much enjoy mechanical theory but I hung on grimly, using all my high school study skills. My notebook fattened with incoherent flow lines and arrows. We sanded and varnished more wood, patched more fabric, relearned the structure of aircraft and the myriad kinds of tools. Words like "spars-and-ribs," "stressed skin," "geodetic frame," and "micrometer" danced in my head. My old friend theory-of-flight was back with "stability, equilibrium, relative airflow, lift and drag, angles of yaw and roll."

I met more rivets than I ever wanted to know: pierced, semi-pierced, snaphead, round head, pan head, mushroom head, and flat head. I became acquainted but never intimate with the lap joint and double butt strap joint. I learned how to put a rivet in, and how to get it out if I messed up.

Periodically there were tests.

> We had an oral exam today. I thought it was hard as did all of them. I never did like orals and the instructors here want a good full answer for everything. I studied 2½ hours for it last night alone. . . . Chuck Howard went to hospital with mumps yesterday. I was patching a wing with him all day so if I miss getting them this time I must have a charmed life. . . .

An early heat wave descended in May. Lawn mowers whirred across the TTS greensward, filling the air with a scent I'd never known (fresh-cut grass was not the same as new-mown hay). Ontario turned an unbelievable emerald green. The lawns and distant fields shimmered in languorous heat—not the dry, ground-baking prairie summer but moist and lush. Semitropical heat. *Rich* people's heat.

Stores issued us RCAF summer dress: tan lightweight uniforms with blue shoulder patches and insignia, worn with our blue wedge caps. Wrinkle-free synthetics were years away. In Ontario's humidity a freshly pressed uniform became a sack in thirty minutes. Each night we spent hours with electric irons, and for an emergency press we slept with our pants under the mattresses, which gave an interesting waffle effect.

Finally TTS turned us loose in the benign outdoors to work on functioning aircraft. My romantic heart soared. Like most of my generation, I had never been on an airplane nor even close to one.

April 28, 1944

> Flight Routine is when we go out to the field where all the ships are lined up and learn how to handle them on the ground. . . . When they start warming up three or four at once it's really deafening. I often wonder what it's like on an airport when they have lines of bombers warming up before a raid. They have a dive bomber in here. They're quite a plane—all camouflaged and fitted with guns, and they have special flaps on the wings for steep dives. . . .

We learned how to wave a pilot onto his spot on the tarmac, how to chock the wheels so the ship wouldn't roll away, and the art of spinning the propeller to start a small plane without losing our arms or heads. Fun at last! Real airplanes at last!

Amidst all the usual RCAF duties I was staunchly enthusiastic and blossoming with new confidence. I wrote in the same letter that P.T. on the velvet green lawns was "fun." We spent a week on Duty Flight, meaning we were confined to barracks at night and assigned a joe-job. I remained cheery.

> We're lucky 'cause we got fire picquet. That means we just have to wait around for something to catch fire. Westy says we can write letters or study or anything at all except leave camp. Suits me okay as we don't go out during the week anyway. And for once I missed getting stuck in the mess hall.

Amazingly, I even liked the station disciplinarian, Flight Sergeant Bruce Shaw, a handsome fellow with a fine clear bugle of a voice. Where others bullied and threw their rank, Shaw had the knack of winning our best effort with air force humor.

"All right, you men, let's *swing* those arms!" he'd cry cheerfully, his voice reverberating across the parade square. "They're hanging there like limp cocks!"

I even volunteered for the monthly drill squad competition, mainly to get extra leave but also because I liked the way we crackled through the drill. Being there *by choice* made all the difference. We were good: arms and legs in perfect unison, feet stamping with a single crash, rifles whipping through intricate new routines. We lost by a few points to the WD's squad, a bitter pill for men to swallow, but I got my seventy-two–hour pass.

On weekends most of us sprinted for the London & Port Stanley railway station just outside camp. When possible we sneaked out wearing nonregulation shirts of a softer lighter hue than the blue-gray air force issue. If the SPs at the guard house bellowed, "WHERE YA THINK YER GOING WITH THAT SHIRT?" we pragmatically went back and changed it.

The L&PS, better known as the Late and Poor Service, was an eighty-eight–year–old electric railway, the butt of many jokes, but a boon to us. Airmen could get six tickets to London for a dollar or to the Lake Erie resort town of Port Stanley for fifty cents.

St. Thomas, a somnolent city of 17,500, did not win our affections; we'd just had Moose Jaw. But it was within easy range of Detroit, Toronto, and, only a half-hour away, London. The last, with its population of 87,000, was rich in restaurants, theaters, beer parlors, a 14,000–square-foot roller skating arena, and, of course, girls.

The important thing about girls was simply *having* or even *seeming* to have one. It was imperative, after a date or two, that she give you her most glamorous picture. You kept it in your wallet, with similar trophies. A special girl went into the miniature snap-shot compartment of your sterling silver identification bracelet. The girls in turn collected *our* photos—we always posed smartly in the 'TEN-SHUN or AT-EASE positions—for their wallets or lockets. Now that my skin was clearing up, I was actually going on dates and entering into this barter.

May 21, 1944

> I think maybe I'll get a picture taken before long. They go around making bargain offers to all the boys and I'm a sucker for a bargain.

Most of us kept ever-expanding rogues' galleries of men friends —women friends from long past, to burnish our reputations. We then boasted to one another about this "grand girl" or "swell guy," and produced evidence. It meant we belonged, were admired, needed, and maybe loved.

The first queen of my wallet was Margie, a sixteen-year-old with dramatic tendencies. Although I was nineteen, it was hard to say which of us was robbing the cradle. At the end of each date she locked me in a fervent embrace that brought the veins to my forehead and a permanent crease to my summer tunic. Then she gasped, "We must stop doing this!" in a line straight from Rita Hayworth or Betty Grable. "This" was merely the pneumatic kiss, an art at which Margie excelled, while arching backwards in my arms like the girl on the White Shoulders perfume bottle.

After a while we stopped doing "it," with no hard feelings on either side, and I dated a small brunette waitress named Marie. She was gentle and loyal: once she came out in pouring rain to watch me and a hundred other soggy airmen march down Dundas Street on some meaningless exercise.

Many times, there were no girls. On one such forlorn Saturday night, two of my friends rented a two-dollar hotel room on a dubious section of Richmond Street, and five more of us sneaked in to spend the night. We were up to no particular mischief. Mainly it just seemed like a hell of a good idea. It was a mild flaunting of rules that I wouldn't have dreamed of a year before. My mother would have disapproved.

We brought along a few beers and planned to sleep sitting up on chairs, or crosswise like rows of cordwood on the single bed. The thumping of fourteen feet soon alerted a night clerk who chased us all into the street. We mooched around until morning, and gratefully returned to the free food and beds at TTS.

Even that night, I probably had a dollar or two squirreled away.

That was my mother's legacy too. I was rarely flat broke. I didn't smoke, drank little, played no poker, and lent money only to reliable friends. Financially, I'd never been better off but was smart enough to not brag about it. The station magazine, *The Aircraftman*, ran an editorial about a creature rarer than the great auk—an AC2 who'd *saved* $120 from his $1.30 a day pay. Mercifully, he was not named, or he'd have been hooted off the station. To be caught saving money was as bizarre and antisocial as having no girlfriend or never having known a hoo-er.

Week nights in barracks were never idle. After lights out, someone usually flushed the long gleaming rows of urinals in quick succession, screaming, "FIRE ONE! FIRE TWO! FIRE THREE! . . ." as each went off like thunder. For those in lower bunks, another antidote for boredom was to wait until the man in the upper dozed off, plant both feet firmly on the underside of his mattress, kick hard, and watch him go straight up.

We told jokes, the most printable concerning the Kee Bird, so named because it flew in ever-increasing spirals, high, high in the sky until it finally screeched, "Kee-kee-kee-KEEE-RIST, IT'S COLD UP HERE!" We "frenched" one another's beds: deftly doubling the bottom sheet back, then impeccably folding and smoothing the covers in place. When the victim sprang in, his feet stopped short halfway down, driving his knees to his chin.

One evening Sam, Haddon, and Eldon fixed their fertile minds on a man who was being married the next weekend. A whisper ran through the bay: "Let's shave his balls!" With several strong men holding him down on his bunk—as he bucked, cursed, and shed a tear or two of rage and humiliation—others lathered and delicately shaved his pubic hair. I helped hold his feet, and afterward felt ashamed. But, although a dirty trick, it did not impair his marriage.

Sometimes we were kind to one another. One night, rushing for a date with Margie the virgin sex fiend, I had no clean shirts. I hastily rinsed one in the sink and raced off to shave. When I returned, the hard-muscled McParland was voluntarily ironing my shirt.

"My mother taught me," he said, humming a little tune as he worked. He didn't need to explain. Nobody was about to challenge McParland on why he knew how to do shirts.

One of our fraternity was Gordon Winton from Hamilton, skinny and short. Like me, he must surely have longed for muscles and style, but he carried on with a jaunty smile and finally won a permanent place in our affections. One weekend a half-dozen of us hitchhiked to the Niagara Peninsula in steaming soggy heat, our uniforms drooping at the elbows and knees. En route through Hamilton, Winton led us to the shady sanctuary of a soda fountain.

"Boys," he said, with an airy wave at the proprietor, "this is my dad. Dad, these are the boys." He paused, and added grandly, "Order anything you like!" .

We were still teenagers enough to envy anybody whose old man ran a soda fountain. Before our respectful eyes, Winton Sr. set up free shakes and cones, and Winton Jr. grew six inches.

The long hard course ended on the last day of June. In the Examination Centre, each of us was quizzed on every phase of his trade by three different examiners. For one hour and ten minutes assorted corporals, sergeants, and flight-sergeants fired 150 to 200 questions at us. It was a draining experience, but not without its lighter moments. An aero engine trainee, when asked "What's it mean when you see blue smoke coming from the exhaust?", rewarded the RCAF for thirty weeks of high-priced training with "It means the engine's running!"

"What's an essential ingredient in a good solder?" they asked a prospective fixer of airframes.

"Alimony!" cried the trainee. He meant antimony.

An engine graduate in an earlier class, Joe Fink of Plunkett, Saskatchewan, later told me he was presented with an unrecognizable (to him) piece of motor during his final TTS.

"Fink, where does this piece go?" said the examiner. Joe was stumped. He stared, sighed, and absently leaned his hand at random on the motor beside them.

"Right!" cried the instructor. "Well done, Fink!"

Out of the fifty-five airframe mechanics in our entry only four flunked. At 8:30 A.M. on July 5 the rest of us lined up—with forty-six aero engine mechanics, thirty instrument mechanics, twelve parachute riggers, and nineteen flight engineers—for the commanding officer's parade. Our pants stayed pressed just long enough for him to wish us farewell and welcome a new incoming entry.

I proudly stitched the airframe badge on my sleeve: a white silhouette of an aircraft on a black background. I was now an AC1, "C" group. My daily pay had soared to $1.65.

It was a watershed in our careers, the first of many poignant partings. Reveling as I was in the new-found breadth and variety of friendships, I realized that in the service they were transitory. At home I had known Walter, Bill, and Elford Bell, in the big farmhouse a mile south, almost as long as I'd known my own brother. After eight years of grade school Clifford Bell and Gilbert Hagstrom were permanent friends. But now a friendship could burn bright for six months, then flicker and die, when the air force sent us in opposite directions.

Each of us got a fourteen-day furlough before reporting to his new posting. Would we ever meet again? Only the air force knew. I and four strangers went to No. 9 Bombing and Gunnery School in Mont Joli, Quebec. Eldon Fairburn was posted to Rockliffe in Ottawa; I would see him only once again during the war. Sam Glassford, reporting to No. 6 Service Flying Training School at Camp Borden north of Toronto, and no letter-writer, dropped from sight for a while.

Reg Starks was sent to Dafoe, Saskatchewan, within easy reach of home. On his two-week leave he married his sweetheart. Not one house was available in the little air force boom town so he and his father moved a thresherman's caboose – a kind of mobile bunkhouse – to Dafoe. That was Reg and Anne Starks's first home. I never saw him again during the war.

I took the train to Shamrock for two glad weeks of food and family. But my head was in the future. Four weeks earlier the Allies had fought their way up the beaches of Normandy. Now the Canadian and British ground forces were fighting for Caen. A massive Allied aerial attack – six thousand sorties in twenty-four hours – had just pounded Hitler's Europe. The Russians were fighting so savagely that even Goebbels, the Nazi propaganda minister, warned the German people of "mortal danger in the east."

If I were ever to do anything useful in this war, it'd better be soon. Now was my chance.

Chapter Six

Wednesday night, July 26, 1944. Canadian Pacific Railway
No. 2 is grunting and snuffling through the Ontario wilder-
ness behind the whistle's keening song. *Wooo-wooo-woo-wooo,*
it cries, in trainmen's code: *public crossing ahead!* Strange little place names, visible only to the quick of eye, flash past
in blurs of feeble light. Whistle stops, too unimportant for
the mainliner. They trail behind us in the dark. . . Loon . . .
Ouimet . . . Black Sturgeon . . . Red Rock . . .

I am stretched full-length on the padded leather bench
seat in the lavatory-smoking compartment of an ancient day
coach. My friend of the moment, a French Canadian army
boy, is asleep on the neighboring seat. Our heads lie inches
away from a foul-smelling brass spittoon but we are happy
as kings. Finding an empty smoker at night is like winning
the Irish Sweepstakes. It's almost as good as a berth, which
neither of us can afford, and infinitely better than sitting
upright in our day coach seats. *Mont Joli, here I come.*

I have been traveling thirty hours, with another sixty to
go. Tonight, on this stretch between Fort William and Sudbury, there are few stops and fewer oncoming passengers.
Blessed peace. We drowse to *clickety-clack chirp-squeak* and
the soothing tattoo of rain on the windows. Better enjoy it,
we tell ourselves. Tomorrow night there'll be crowds again
and the smoker will be full of smoking, hacking, spitting,
joke-swapping, lie-telling men and a mickey of rotgut rye
whiskey passing from hand to hand. We'll be propped up
back in the day coach with rented pillows, aching to the mar-
row of our bones and sleeping by fits and starts among crying kids and the sickly smell of stale orange peel. . . .

Trains were my second home. They took us everywhere that trucks could not. Throughout the war I never set foot in an automobile except on leave. After eighteen years of only once being on a train, my life was suddenly a blur of cavernous stations, with disembodied voices calling out: "The Dominion . . . now boarding on track three for Winnipeg, Kenora, Port Arthur, Sudbury, Montreal . . ."

Trains, trains, always trains. The mad merry clang of the bell and the hiss of steam as they pulled into a station. The billow of inky black trailing out from the smokestack. Marching at night through pools of yellow street light to yet another train, while normal folk slumbered. Seeing Canada in train-window cameos: Saskatchewan's shadowy grain elevators flickering past in silver moonlight, the vast metallic shimmer of Lake Superior, a sooty jungle of Toronto smokestacks. Gulping the news vendors' doughy sandwiches and fierce black coffee. Rolling down the aisle with a sailor's gait. Hacking your chin with a razor in the smoker as the train pitched and lurched; crashing nose first into the mirror at a sudden grinding stop. Singing, to the tune of "Humoresque," the CPR's scolding notice riveted above the toilet seat:

> Passengers will please refrain
> From flushing toilets while the train
> Is standing in the station
> In full view . . .

Now the trains were chugging me through Broadview, Virden, Wabigoon, Ignace, Schreiber, White River, Chapleau . . . and, for the first time, into Quebec Province. Almost a foreign land.

Back home, the town of Gravelbourg, sixteen miles away, was a predominantly French oasis on the prairie. It offered a rare opportunity to sample another culture, but we went there strictly for English-language movies, the doctor, and the Chinese restaurant. I knew no Francophones. We had nothing against them except that they spoke French. My father, who treasured his prejudices, called them Peasoups. So did I and everyone else in the neighborhood, except Christians like my mother.

Now I'd encountered a French Canadian who, admittedly, was a nice guy. But my first letter home still showed more interest in Quebec's railway stations than its people:

July 29, 1944

We reached Montreal at 6:45 on Friday morning, and with the aid

59

of my French Canadian friend and a passing Peasoup, I found my way to the CNR station. They have beautiful stations down here—everything from soup to nuts. I went into the lovely big washroom. It was quite a treat to shave with a steady hand and no danger of by-passing a couple of veins. Then I went to the Canadian Legion War Services room and found lots of kindly old ladies who bustled around and fixed me a cot and arranged to wake me up whenever I wanted to be roused. I had a couple of hours' sleep in a lovely cool shaded room on a nice clean cot and it sure was a godsend. It's absolutely free to all service personnel. . . .

At noon I caught an eastbound train. Lilting place names in French accents trailed behind me in the station: "Levis . . . Riviere-du-Loup . . . Rimouski . . ." The French tongue welled up around me. Like most Anglos of my time and place, I had been taught French by teachers who'd never heard it spoken. We memorized words and grammar. Not once did we hear the music and rhythm of the language. It was worse than *no* instruction because it left me with a mental block and a wooden tongue.

But now, as my long journey faded into its last night, Quebec began to beguile me.

I must say it's really pretty in places. Quebec looks just like the history books made me expect—tiny little farms with the farmhouses thick as fleas, lots of green rolling land with lovely rich hay meadows, and regular old-fashioned log fences in lots of places. . . . Speaking of logs, Dad, have you piled all the fence posts yet? Just think, last Saturday I was home piling posts and tonight I'm down here right in the middle of the swamp-singers [frogs]. Join the air force and see the world, they say.

At 1 A.M. I detrained at Mont Joli's small station with a handful of equally bewildered flight engineers, phoned camp for a truck, and went through the arrival ritual.

First we went to the SPs. These brave young men gloated over our passes, asked numerous unnecessary questions, ogled us lovingly all the while, and after finally deciding that we were not members of the Gestapo in disguise, reluctantly let us go to bed. We were put in an empty room with some cots and mattresses. Some poor souls had no blankets and slept between two mattresses. . . .

In the morning, trudging from high to low—officers to sergeants—I got signatures on necessary forms and found a permanent bunk. The barracks were like most others across Canada: frame outside, bilious green inside. Some sweet-talking green paint salesman had sold the air force a trainload.

That afternoon I helped put a wing on a plane. My contribution was minimal but at last I was doing *real* war work! This was a genuine working aircraft, used to train air crews—not a stripped-down skeleton in Wet-Pee or TTS. For the first time in a year, I went to bed with a sense of purpose.

The regimen was twenty-four days on, four days off, but the next day, a Sunday, was an unexpected holiday. It looked "sinister," I wrote my parents, tongue in cheek; the air force never gives you something for nothing. In fact, it was a reward to the entire station for setting an all-time record in July: 6,406 hours and 15 minutes of flying time.

Compared with Brandon and St. Thomas, the base was like a cosy town: a mere 2,200 officers, airmen and airwomen, civilian employees, and student air gunners and flight engineers. Most of its 110 aircraft were Fairey Battles, a metal low-wing single-engine day bomber that had served the RAF in France in the earliest months of the war. The crew sat in-line under a plastic canopy, pilot up front, gunner facing the rear. It could cruise 900 miles at 220 miles per hour with a thousand-pound bomb load. By 1944 its forty-foot length and forty-two–foot wingspan were dwarfed by the mammoths bombing Germany, but the Battle was a durable training craft and, to me, a thing of wonder.

On clear days the station crackled with action. Pilots with parachute packs flapping over their rear ends as they strolled to the planes. Armorers checking the machine guns. Student gunners taking their seats, as nervous in their new jobs as I was in mine. Motors revving and thrumming. Battles taking off and landing. In the sky, planes trailing behind them the "drogues" that the gunners would use as targets. Air scented with gasoline and glycol. All of it exhilarating! But August turned out rainy, a disappointing month for flying. An opportunity to get acquainted with the station and the town.

Mont Joli itself was just another parochial Quebec town. We Anglos felt unwelcome amid its indifferent stares, and went there only to catch the outbound train. The conscription issue was tearing Canada apart that autumn. In Europe, the army badly needed reinforcements. The only obvious source in Canada was the Zombies, seventy thousand home-service conscripts who refused to volunteer for overseas. Some were conscientious objectors. A sizable proportion were Quebecers, bitterly opposed to fighting a "British" war. We Anglos, particularly from the West, tended to think *all* Zombies were French. "Bloody Peasoups won't fight!" my father growled.

All of this inflamed my prejudices toward the town and its inhabitants.

August 5, 1944

> They have two bowling alleys which make up the town's entertainment. One is inhabited by the air force and the other by the local Tough Eggs. I understand that in the latter they don't set up pins but just square off and let fly at each other. Incidentally, Quebec is full of big healthy guys who'd make great cannon fodder. . . .

Yet our barracks were full of another kind of Francophone, brothers in arms and ordinary guys like me. We were all volunteers, in for the duration, happy in the service together. The nights were full of shouts in French, English, and *Franglaise*. I noted with interest and envy that they went faithfully to Mass and confession each Sunday (we Protestants were indifferent churchgoers), and then seemed to have a clear run at sin for the rest of the week.

They tended to chum with one another, largely because of language (they all spoke English to some extent but few of us had French), but we razzed one another impartially, the way East and West had done at Manning.

The station offered two French courses (one for officers, one for Other Ranks). I sent home for my high school French text and dictionary and signed up in another attempt to learn the language. I managed to master two good swearwords: *"Câlise!"* and *"Tabernac!"*

"Tab-errnac!" I would offer tentatively (so much more stylish than English swearing, I thought).

"*Câlise*, Col-lins!" a French voice from some neighboring bunk would cry in mock despair at my accent.

My favorite Francophone was Guertin, short, ebullient, fluently bilingual, with good schooling and a great toothy grin. We laughed a lot together. When we finally left the base, I snapped a farewell gag shot of him—his wedge cap square amidships, his hand tucked formally into the front of his greatcoat—posing as Napoleon. After that I never spoke of Peasoups or swamp-singers.

I rid myself of another myth: that women were in uniform to

serve as vehicles of pleasure for officers. The WDs on our station did every conceivable job from driving trucks to patching
planes, and did them well. They came from farms and villages
and every imaginable background, just like us. They could be
as lonely as we, or more so. There was an aching isolation to being
a plain girl in a plain uniform, stranded on the sidelines at a dance
while men—who always did the asking—converged on civilian
girls in frilly dresses.

The WDs not only worked skillfully and hard but their cheery
feminine presence—as a senior officer once put it—"raised the tone
of the mess." What he meant was, because of the women we
arrived for meals combed and brushed, and behaved more like
gentlemen and less like slobs.

Outside the mess hall . . . well, some were more gentlemanly
than others. Certain airmen spent hours hunched over pieces of
the plastic used in Fairey Battle canopies, cutting and polishing
small translucent heart-shaped plastic brooches with the RCAF
crest embedded. These were popular gifts for wives back home,
symbols of undying love from husbands who were cheating on
them in Quebec.

Others whiled away whole evenings discussing the ethical pros
and cons of bedding virgins versus married women. Generally,
married men favored deflowering virgins. Fooling around with
other men's wives was immoral, they said virtuously (haunted,
as they were, by images of other men seducing *their* wives back
home). Preying on innocent virgins? Scandalous, I thought! Married women were fair game; they knew what they were getting
into, or vice versa. My views, of course, were strictly based on
theory.

Sometimes we drifted to the drill hall to play basketball, punch
the heavy bag or the speed bag, or listen to a certain leading aircraftman play the battered upright piano. He was a moody close-
mouthed fellow but popular music and classics poured from his
fingers. Most nights, a few of us hovered around, quietly making requests. As long as we weren't pushy, he seemed to enjoy
our company. He played a magnificent rolling boogie-woogie, and
his rendition of the "Warsaw Concerto" became a feature of these
impromptu concerts.

One night a young flying officer strolled over with his girl. We
glanced up and went on listening to the latest hit, "Don't Fence
Me In." Officially, officers and Other Ranks didn't fraternize. We
did not share the air crew–ground crew camaraderie of the oper-

ational air force overseas. Here, we didn't work with the same pilot and airplane, day after day. I viewed officers with mingled fear (Manning Depot had firmly established them as figures of authority) and envy. Even the best of them exuded an indefinable air of superiority. I resented touching my forelock to someone who by luck of the draw, a better education, or better color vision had rings on his sleeve.

Nevertheless, the officers and NCOs here, as on most working stations, were a different breed from those in training. There was still a distinct pecking order—the air force would never be a democracy—but the sergeants and corporals were not martinets and the air crew officers were not salute-happy. Neither were we erks. During off-duty hours, on our own turf, we no longer sprang to attention for anything less than a wing commander.

"How about 'Warsaw Concerto'?" asked the F/O, politely but with the unmistakable tone of one used to receiving the undivided attention of Other Ranks. The LAC ignored him for several bars, then said softly without looking up, "I don't know it."

It was an awkward moment—he was famous for the number— but there was nothing the officer could do. The message, although petty, was clear: the airman took orders all day but at night he ran his own piano.

The F/O shrugged, trying to save face, and turned away with his girl. Just as they reached the door there was a crash of chords—and the "Warsaw Concerto" filled the drill hall as never before. The couple listened from a respectful distance. The temperamental LAC had made his point: *I'm a person, not a rank.*

Bill Steppler and I exchanged grins. Steppler, from Vancouver, was my newest and closest pal. He was my age, short and handsome with curly hair, a soft voice, and a merry disposition. As a former corporal in the Pacific Coast militia, he came to the air force knowing what I was still learning the hard way: how to get around the military. I warmed to him immediately. His mind was always busy. His entrepreneurism seemed to complement my creative bent. Together, we were always up to something.

Steppler was very strong in the arms and shoulders—he'd shown me how to hammer a rat-a-tat-tat on the speed bag in the gym—but his height and mild demeanor caused bigger men to underestimate him. One such was Big Louie, the barracks practical joker, a towering youth with an angelic smile and the mind of a naughty small boy. One night outside the showers Louie was enjoying his favorite sport: snapping bare buttocks with the end of a wet towel. He laid a sharp one on Steppler. One snap was considered fair game. Louie did it twice.

"Don't do that again, Louie," Steppler said gently. Louie did. Steppler went for him. It was five-foot-six versus six-foot-four, which seemed to be no contest. Louie bounced Steppler off the wall but on the rebound Steppler yanked the other's feet, bringing his head down hard on a metal bunk. The blow, enough to fell a giant redwood, actually stunned Big Louie. Instantly Steppler got him in an armlock that even Louie couldn't break. They called it a draw. Louie never bothered him again.

Steppler had a flair for airframe. He'd graduated from TTS with a "B" grouping (compared to my run-of-the-mill "C") and at Mont Joli was put on Maintenance doing important major repairs. I was passed from hand to hand like the cat nobody wants.

I served a stint on the flight line, tending planes before takeoff and after landing, checking for damage and refueling them from a truck called a bowser. For ground crew, flight line was the action center of No. 9 B&G. I found it enthralling and terrifying by turns. I loved the idea of being around aircraft but now I was *responsible* for them.

I had no affinity for machines. There'd been only one motor of any kind on our farm, the 1929 Chev, and neither my father nor I understood it. Here, in airframe, motors weren't my concern, but there were dozens of other moving parts—trim tabs, ailerons, hydraulic brakes, shock absorbers. Being painfully conscientious, but with faint confidence in my training (much of it seemed irrelevant on the flight line), I was constantly afraid of goofing up. The station won another holiday for record flying time in September—6,095 hours and 25 minutes—but I felt I'd done nothing to earn it.

Autumn rain and fog were common along the St. Lawrence, only a mile or so away. On October 1, a Battle went down, injuring three men. Six days later, two more crashed beyond repair, killing a pilot and three student gunners and seriously injuring a fourth.

This *was* wartime, we *were* in the military; but for most it was our first brush with violent death and it cast a pall over the station for a few days. I knew none of the dead or injured. I was not on the flight line at the time. But the thought haunted me: *What if I failed to fix something and caused a crash?* Still, it was necessary war work and I doggedly kept at it as best I could. It was better than being demoted to kitchen helper.

The "96s"—four-day leaves—were a blessed relief. On one of them, Steppler and I discovered Ottawa. I sent home a glowing fourteen-page catalogue of wonders: the Parliament Buildings "with a huge very lovely library that a person could spend a year browsing through," the Cenotaph, our rooming house with an "absolutely perfect" room for a dollar a night, the movie *Since You Went Away* ("a lot of people came out bawling"), the service canteen ("very good food at very low prices"), and Mackenzie King who appeared at a November 11 ceremony ("just like his pictures except a little more doddering if possible").

We saw a concert with a "swell violinist" playing "Ave Maria," and attended a free Sadie Hawkins dance heavily populated by civil service girls who all said they hated Mackenzie King. I ventured timidly onto the floor. They seemed not to mind the relentless one-two-one-two shuffle that was my version of waltz, rhumba, polka, and jitterbug.

On the way back we stopped a day in Montreal. We were broke, but struck gold at a serviceman's center: two free tickets to a businessmen's lunch that noon. We performed the ritual: stood when bidden, announced our names and home towns, and tucked gratefully into the main course. We ate everything in sight, enough to get us back to Mont Joli.

Usually, on a "96," we took the train to Campbellton, New Brunswick, a friendly town of 7,500, a hundred miles east. Steppler and I always checked into the Salvation Army hostel. Then we'd climb Sugarloaf Mountain or go on a wiener roast or try a local dance. Once we went to church, where our blue uniforms were so rare a sight that the minister welcomed us from the pulpit. We ducked our heads modestly. We were not really worthy of his praise. How could an airman be pure in heart, surrounded as he was by provocation?

I will call her Jenny Lavoie, which is the only fictional name in this book. Somewhere, I hope, she is living in grandmotherly contentment with those memories far behind her. Every servicemen's town had a Jenny Lavoie. Ours was in her late teens or early twenties, with a magnificent body, dark hair, dark eyes, and a hard-edged ebullience that probably masked a lot of emotional scars.

I met her, as other men did, at a local joint where airmen and civilian girls hung out for coffee and Cokes. I liked her bold open manner and her sense of humor; she was easy to talk to and her presence was exciting. I enjoyed the invitation of her too-tight skirts and tighter sweaters although hadn't the slightest intention of doing anything about it. I was still too much a product of Shamrock, Saskatchewan. Anyway, to be seen with Jenny could ruin one's reputation with the "nice" girls in town, two of whom Steppler and I were dating sporadically. In those times only "bad" girls or outright prostitutes openly slept around.

Jenny did not sell her body. She gave it away, to anyone who asked her nicely. I thought she was either a nymphomaniac (I'd never met one but wanted to) or extremely friendly. Now, I suppose that she, like everyone else of that time, was looking for love the best way she knew how.

One night a few of us went to a local barn dance. It was not much like the rural version in Standon School back home, where a square dance was an intricate weaving and swirling of dancers while Butch Gwin, our barrel-bellied caller, boomed his ritual instructions: "NOW BIRDY FLY OUT AND BIRDY FLY IN . . . SWING YER PARTNERS, CORNERS ALL AND DOSEY DOH."

In Campbellton this night, men and women lined up on opposite sides of the hall and seemed to charge one another in a melee of bodies, while the fiddles screamed their lovely manic tunes. I had never mastered the prairie square dance but here, lubricated with a mickey of Seagram's 83 and presented with simpler steps, Old Lead-Foot turned into a backwoods Fred Astaire. After a while I realized that Jenny Lavoie was dancing with me, her spectacular breasts boring into my blue chest.

"It's so hot in here," she said when the music stopped. "Let's go out and cool off."

I was much hotter than she guessed. She led me onto a nearby hillside in the autumn night.

"Let's sit down."

"Okay. Oh . . . *yeah!*"

"It's kind of damp; why don't you spread your raincoat?" asked Jenny Lavoie helpfully. Dumbly, obediently, I did. Every prudent airman carried his blue plastic raincoat or rubber groundsheet at all times, in case of sudden rain or sex. We sank onto it. I was not too dense to know what was going on. This was every man's fantasy: a comely promiscuous girl was coming on to *me!* We kissed enthusiastically and Jenny Lavoie's splendid body moved invitingly. The next move was obviously mine.

And then the medical officer and his bloody films loomed into my line of vision, figuratively speaking. For nearly a year, his kind

67

had terrified me and other impressionable airmen with threats of VD.

"You go dipping your wick into the first easy lay and it's gonna fall right off," they had warned. They offered unlimited hand-outs of contraceptives but I shrank from asking and enduring the orderlies' sly grins.

Now, as I lay panting on a New Brunswick hillside with this willing and able girl, maimed and tortured penises from the MO's films marched in four-color before my mind's eye. After some more kissing I lifted Jenny Lavoie and my raincoat and took them both back to the dance. She was visibly annoyed.

A few weeks later we were back in Campbellton. A sailor checked into the hostel. He was an easy breezy fellow, more worldly than we but not so chippy as many of his kind. He hummed a little tune as he unpacked his kit. He pronounced this a "pusser hostel," meaning in navy slang that it was excellent, first class, the genuine article. Then, courteously—rather like a tourist seeking directions to the Peace Tower or Big Ben—he said he was looking for a sure thing and did we have any recom-mendations.

He was a stranger in town and we were regulars—hell, *hosts*, almost. "Jenny Lavoie!" we chorused, and gave directions. Later I was ashamed for helping turn Jenny into a tourist attraction (although there was no evidence that she minded).

Most of all, I was jealous.

Chapter Seven

Now I was sweeping hangar floors and cleaning up oil spills with varsol, under the cold eye of Bert Lusher, a tall LAC with a bony face and imperious manner. I disliked him intensely and the feeling was mutual because, sometimes, I challenged his curt orders. This mild rebellion was unlike me. Slowly but perceptibly, I was crawling out of my shell. In part it came from hanging around with the irrepressible Steppler.

I was bored. I liked working with my hands if it meant inventing or improvising, and had hoped airframe might indulge this bent. If I could not be a hero, let me be a tinker. Now it was clear I would never be more than an aerial service station attendant. I would gas up planes, check cockpits for cobwebs, kick tires for flats. I would do everything except wash the windshield and tell the pilot to have a nice day.

Early in December I visited the station counsellor. His job was to offer wisdom to career-troubled souls.

"What do you want to be when you get out?" he asked.

"A journalist."

That stumped him. He gave me tests. Not much had changed. Again I scored a high 71 on the RCAF classification test, plus 142 on a clerical aptitude test and a dismal 35 on mechanical knowledge.

"Tested and classified," he wrote in his report. "Encouraged to carry on. Seems like a quiet type. Inclined to be self-conscious. I suggested he try to be more agressive [sic]. Borrowed book."

I carried on. One day I begged a plane ride. Mechanics could go up if there was a spare seat, and get seventy-five cents flying pay to boot. I buckled on a parachute and joined the pilot of a small Nomad circling over snowy fields and the great St. Lawrence for a glorious half-hour.

"First flip?" he said pleasantly. I nodded. In fact, it would be the only one of my air force career. There was no sense of fear (I had more faith in the pilot and other mechanics than in myself). Nor was I airsick. For a few wistful moments, I wished I were in air crew. Like Roy Bien. Like F/O Buzz Beurling, hero of Malta. Like Wing Commander Guy Gibson of the Dambusters.

Back on earth I was promoted to the radiator shop, a cosy nook with a door that closed, in the corner of a hangar. Fairey Battle radiators regularly blew leaks in their honeycomb surfaces. I joined Gabe, a devil-may-care dude from Sault Ste. Marie, in the agreeable task of finding the leaks by bubbling high-pressure air through the rads underwater, preparing them with flux, patching them with hot solder, and testing them underwater again. If no bubbles came up, we'd done our job. We were good at it.

Gabe and I ran our own show and had many visitors. He was a witty popular fellow, with the aquiline profile and hungry good looks of Leslie Howard in *Gone with the Wind*. I was gaining weight and looked less like an ad for an acne cure. Often the WDs from the fabric shop came in for tea and sticky buns. Our favorite was Bonnie, a pretty laughing girl whose heroic bust popped the buttons on her air force coveralls.

Life became tolerable, but Steppler and I had long ago volunteered for the next overseas draft. Technically, we all were subject to overseas posting at any time, but now we had to take the initiative. The Russians were nearing Budapest. Most of France had been freed. The Nazis had just mounted a stiff counteroffensive in the Ardennes but an Allied victory sometime in 1945 seemed likely. Establishments were snapping shut behind us. Brandon Manning Depot had closed the previous May; Wet-Pee Moose Jaw in July.

On Christmas morning I went to the Protestant chapel. It wasn't much like Wiwa Hill Anglican Church south of Shamrock, with the intimacy of a small congregation, sunlight filtering softly onto the fourteen pews, children's piping voices raised in hymns. But this church was better than no church on my first Christmas away from home.

Our mess hall, with its bare overhead girders and bare bulbs hanging from tin shades, had a skinny pathetic artificial wreath in each window. Dinner was plenty of turkey with the usual trimmings, mince pie, plum pudding, fruit and candy, cigarettes, Coke, and beer. But it was a raucous affair and I was in a sour puritanical mood (probably exaggerated, in my letter, to win brownie points with my teetotaling mother).

> December 26, 1944
>
> They make a mistake giving out free beer at a dinner like that. For about fifty percent of the men who are deadbeats anyway, it's a glorious chance to get a glow on at the air force's expense. They hide away their beer and go back for more, fill their pockets with oranges and anything else that's not tied down. The result was a riproaring drinking party. The officers and senior NCOs did the serving and did a pretty good job. But before they began they had blotted up a few pints of beer and most of them couldn't see straight. . . .

We had more turkey for the evening meal and smuggled two platefuls to our bunks for bedtime. My parents had shipped cookies, canned chicken, and a cake. Others around me had parcels from home too. Together, swapping and sharing, we ate our way into Boxing Day.

On the thirtieth, Steppler and I took a five-day leave in New York City. We found a room at $1.25 a night (grumbling about the sixteen cents' exchange on the U.S. dollar) and saw everything from the Empire State Building, the Statue of Liberty, and the Automat to Woody Herman live at the Paramount Theatre for fifty cents.

At the world-famous Stage Door Canteen, suave GIs did unbelievable dance steps with glossy hostesses. "They give dandy free food but the dancing was far above most of us," I reported home. In fact, the puzzled hostesses tried repeatedly to drag us onto this most hallowed dance floor in GI America. ("Don't you *want* to dance in the Stage Door Canteen?!" "Uh . . . no, not right now, thanks . . .")

The highlight for me was a tour of Radio City and NBC. I recorded it in ten ecstatic pages.

> January 4, 1945
>
> Best of all, they showed us television. They showed how it was photographed, then took us into a dark room where they had three radio sets equipped with television screens. Some of us went up before the television cameras. The result was perfect, just like a little impromptu movie on your own radio. So far it is only effective at a range of fifty miles but they say that after the war, about three or four years after, it should be within reach of all Canada and the U.S.A. . . . It was a lovely tour and I could see it again any day. This darn radio stuff fascinates me. . . .

As always, my letters were self-censored, to spare the home folks from the true rigors of war. So, I never told them how on New Year's Eve, in the delirium of Times Square, two other airmen and I picked up three girls. Steppler did not. A little later, the six of us met him drifting alone down Broadway. We had no time to commiserate.

"See ya, Stepp," we said cruelly, and kept moving. It was important to maintain momentum at such times. We had *New York* girls, we were going back to their apartment, and we had to strike while they (we hoped) were hot.

These girls were not beautiful, which pleased us. The mythology of the times stated that homely girls were easy to get into bed because they were so grateful. With wild abandon, I joined the others in casting VD paranoia to the winds. We exchanged meaningful smirks. This was IT.

If we had looked deeply into these young women's wise old eyes we would have seen reality. We would have known that in an earlier life they'd been at the building of the Pyramids but had gotten out of carrying heavy loads; had been caught in the Rape of Carthage but emerged with their virginity intact. We would have known that, in their present incarnation, they had repelled endless waves of lustful American GIs and never so much as mussed a pincurl. No trio of RCAF junior ground crew was going to lay a finger on these girls.

We saw them home to a tiny apartment in some distant god-forsaken part of the Bronx, played records, drank bourbon, and half-heartedly tried to get into their pants. It was no contest. They fended us off without missing one crack or snap of their Wrigley's Juicy Fruit. At sunup we parted amicably, blearily rode the subway back to our digs, and slept until noon.

That afternoon, red eyed and with a mouth like the bottom of a bird cage, I went to the New York public library. I loved libraries and this was one of the world's greatest.

Steppler, bright and disgustingly cheerful from a good night's sleep, came along. We stood hushed on its carpeted floors, among its reading rooms with individual lamps. We were surprised at the scores of people – but not one other Canadian serviceman – spending New Year's Day there.

"It would be an ideal place to study," I wrote my family wistfully. It *was* an ideal way to begin 1945.

Chapter Eight

The year was off to a happy start. In January our warrant officer, A. C. Drolet, a bulky man with a Buddha's smile, sent his senior officer a memorandum concerning AC1 Collins, R. J., R270747: "A hard worker. Recommended for reclassification." I passed the necessary trades test. Effective April 1, I'd be promoted to "B" group and to leading aircraftman.

It raised my pay to $2 a day, $730 a year. I would be *rich* – and at last I'd have a rank on my sleeves: the leading aircraftman's horizontal white propeller. Most ground crew were LACs; the props on my tunic would make me one of the gang. As a mechanic hanging onto the job by his fingernails, I didn't aspire to more.

It was a bitter winter. Eastern Quebec dwindled into a Krieghoff miniature with sleighs and plodding horses and muffled fur men creeping across a stark frozen landscape. Constant snow cut flying time to a minimum in January. In mid-February a blizzard blocked the runways for four days. Even the roads in camp were almost impassable. We were ordered to not leave the station, nor even move from building to building in groups of fewer than three.

Inside this white cocoon, strangely detached from the outside world, we moved from barracks to mess hall to hangars while the Mills Brothers softly crooned "I'll Be Around" and the tremulous voice of The Ink Spots' Bill Kenny soared over the P.A. in "If I Didn't Care."

I flung out nets of words and reeled in replies: from my mother's sisters, Aunt Nell in Michigan and Aunt Ferne in the minuscule village of Senate, Saskatchewan. From cousin Eileen on the Collins side, a witty letter from Saskatoon. She'd kept her sense of humor even though her marriage, to an RAF trainee, was falling apart. Bob Sisterson wrote from his base in Manitoba. *Sixteen months ago in Manning he seemed so mature and worldly, beyond my reach. Now we are friends and equals.* Had he changed? No, the change was in me.

Another friend from training, Al Cooper, wrote after a month in England that he didn't like its rainy weather, plain food, or poor living quarters. He envied us, he said. And we envied him.

January 8, 1945

According to rumor number umpteen hundred and one, we will all be posted to India in the coming month. The station will definitely undergo a change by March, so the CO said. So that, coming straight from the kennel, is fairly reliable.

And then, one Saturday morning, a string of names broke through a Frank Sinatra ballad on the hangar loudspeakers. Collins! Guertin! Steppler! I dropped a Fairey Battle radiator in the water tank and ran for the orderly room. Steppler met me on the way. We exchanged jubilant yells. This was it: the overseas draft. Not India but England. And then? Nobody knew. The Russians had just taken Budapest but the western Allies were still meeting fierce German resistance and had not yet reached the Rhine. The war wasn't over, and *at last* we were getting closer.

In the orderly room WO1 Drolet dealt out our papers, beaming like a father. By now he was well acquainted with Steppler and me, the restless ones. We beamed back. Suddenly he was our buddy. Goodbye, Drolet. Good riddance, Lusher.

We signed forms acknowledging that we might be needed for "second phase duty"—the continent, the Pacific, or any other place that pleased His Majesty. The MO examined our lily-white bodies yet again and, over five days, fired two typhus shots into us. We gleefully exchanged our wrinkled summer uniforms for blue battle dress. It cried out "overseas!" because ground crew in Canada never wore it. It also flattered every man's figure. The blouse-tunic with its side buckle at the waist seemed to broaden shoulders and chests and nip emerging bellies. The trousers had a jaunty patch pocket on the left front thigh, for heroes to carry their maps in. And there was not one scrap of despicable brass to polish.

I rushed back to my bunk and sewed the white-lettered "Canada" patches onto my blue shoulders. It was my proudest moment in the RCAF. For the rest of my service I would be entitled to wear them. To the home folks it meant the wearer had served overseas. To people abroad the Canada patch instantly identified us as natives of that most favored and popular of countries. I jumped the gun and sewed on my LAC props too.

Our fourteen days' embarkation leave, including travel time, gave me a week at home. Enough time to say goodbye to my family, and the few other people around Shamrock who cared. Mister Adams. My cousins the Veseys. Auntie May Walker, the dear indomitable English farm neighbor, surrogate aunt to all us kids.

Time enough to be plied with home cooking. To have my picture taken in battle dress, grinning smugly from ear to ear, hair worn a little fuller now, acne gone, shirt fitting neatly at the neck. Feeling good.

The war was hard on parents and wives and brothers and sisters at home. They could only wait and wonder. There was no real reason in February 1945 to fear I would come to harm, but my parents could not be sure. German jets and V-bombs were pounding Britain, and were within a whisker of prolonging the war or even changing its outcome. The mere fact of my crossing the Atlantic was an extraordinary happening in our uneventful lives.

My mother washed my shirts, mended my socks, and tried not to be glum. There was no need for wrenching last words. We all knew each other's hearts. We skirted the underlying fears.

"Do you know when you'll sail, Son?"

"No. Anyway, we're not supposed to tell, when we do. Y'know, censorship. But I'll try to get word to you somehow."

"And you'll be sure to let us know when you get there safe?"

"Soon as I have a chance. But it'll take at least a week to get over, so don't expect anything for maybe ten days."

"Anyway, you'll see Kitty," my father said, and we all brightened. Kitty was his oldest sister in England and our favorite aunt. My father hadn't seen her since he left the Old Country as a first-war convalescent, twenty-eight years before. The rest of us had never seen her, but for twenty-eight years her letters had kept her image bright. My father's eyes said that he envied my trip.

On a Thursday morning, my mother said her farewell at the back door, fighting back her tears and pressing another mighty lunch into my hands. My father walked me through the snow along the tracks to the train.

Seeing someone off at our branch line station was a form of Chinese water torture. The train was always late. When it finally came, the crew ambled, gossiped, shunted a few boxcars, and made it later. Passengers and their stay-at-home loved ones fidgeted on the wooden platform, or in the cramped waiting room with its chattering telegraph, fumbling for something to say when it all had been said.

"You take care of yourself, now, Son."

"Yeah, sure I will. And you too. And don't worry, huh?"

Finally you climbed on, found a seat, looked out and waved. On the platform your next of kin waved back and smiled. You looked away, looked down, adjusted your suitcase. Out there, they looked down, shuffled their feet, looked up Main Street, looked back at the train. You caught one another's eyes, smiled again, waved foolishly (although the train was still rooted to the tracks, perhaps forever), and looked back up Main Street, which had changed very little in the previous sixty seconds. At last the train groaned and chuffed away and you smiled and waved one last time, with mingled tears and relief.

My father, who never backed away from anything in his life, stuck it out through this ordeal, wearing what we called his "fighting face": jaw set, shaggy eyebrows lowering, blue eyes grim. But his love and pride and worry showed through in the way he gripped my hand. Butch Gwin, our grizzled old bachelor neighbor, an uneducated diamond in the rough and friend for as long as I could remember, came to say goodbye. We strove to be casual.

"Well, so long, Butch. Be seeing you."

"You watch out fer them English girls, eh? Har, har!"

Then Tommy Hawkins, renter of our farm, sprang on board to wish me luck. I was surprised and touched. Tommy was tough as boot leather, perpetually sun-tanned and wind-burned, a workaholic who begrudged hours spent away from his fields and barns. He was several years older and, I thought, regarded me as a cream puff. I'd felt uneasy about him since the time in grade school when he hoisted me off the ground by my head; it was called "seeing Paris" because it made you black out.

But now we shook hands with real emotion. I looked back at all of them as the train pulled out, swallowing the lump in my throat. *When would we meet again?*

Four days later I rallied with Steppler and the rest—Sam Glassford was there—at No. 1 "Y" Depot in Moncton. Our departure date was still secret, but in five days we moved to Halifax. We were under strict instructions to not tip off the Nazis so, brimming with intrigue, I mailed a postcard home in code: "Going to see Aunt Kitty tonight. Will write again soon. Lots of love . . ."

The secrecy was perhaps unnecessary. Any self-respecting spy could have sat on a hill in Halifax and figured out that a troop ship was loading. And, in those dying months of the war, the tattered remnants of Hitler's submarine fleet presumably had bigger fish than us to fry. But I was far too conscientious to risk endangering an Allied ship, particularly if I was on it.

We marched straight from the train, through engine smoke and murky light and harbor smells to the dockyard next door. The twenty-year-old *Aquitania*, once a Cunard White Star luxury liner, was waiting for us. To me, she was an astonishing sight—a 45,000-tonner with four smokestacks for her steam turbine engines and four decks, stripped down to handle troops and fitted with submarine-detection gear. She had carried the Canadian Army's First Division overseas in December 1939, and had faithfully plodded the Atlantic ever since with cargoes like us.

As usual, it was late at night, and moving by night had long since lost its romance for me. There was no singing nor undue chatter as we boarded, single file, a winding blue snake lugging the ubiquitous kit bags. I had no particular affection for boats, never having been on one, but the thrill of boarding this mammoth was undeniable. It was a solemn moment—neither scary nor particularly jubilant. We were heading for the unknown, and our biggest adventure.

A band was playing on shore. "Nice of them to see us off," Steppler and I told ourselves. Then we realized they were welcoming a newly arrived hospital ship. As we went up our gangplank, wounded heroes were coming down theirs.

"You'll be *sooorry!*" they yelled, in the servicemen's traditional razzing of greenhorns. Except these men *meant* it. As we went below, my last glimpse of harbor was a sign on a dock shed wall: WELCOME HOME TO CANADA. As usual I was a step behind the war.

The ship was crammed. We shared it with a contingent of Zombies. The conscription order had been passed, in a tumult of outrage and demonstrations, and a few thousand of them began trickling overseas. There were no incidents between them and us. We were literally all in the same boat now.

Alphabetically, as always, we labored with our kit bags deep down into the *Aquitania's* fetid innards, the NCOs herding us on. I ended up on the third deck, squeezed among narrow aisles, and grabbed the first available spot in the multiple tiers of hammocks. Eventually I slept fitfully amid the subdued murmur of other men – it was like the Horse Palace with stale air – and deep in the black night I felt a shudder of engines. The *Aquitania* was easing out to sea.

The next day I located Sam and Steppler and other scattered friends. We had one lifeboat drill. From then on we played hearts and cribbage and poker, tried to dodge joe-jobs, slept fitfully, and prayed for land.

Early that morning, I elbowed through the uniforms on deck and took my first look at the Atlantic from the bow. There were no other vessels around us. Just the gray waters rolling to infinity, not unlike my prairie fields lying somewhere far behind our widening wake. The sight soon lost its charm as the crossing began to get rough.

In Moncton I had stocked up on things that wise men said would win the everlasting gratitude of British girls, all allegedly starved for North American sex and consumer goods. I packed crimson nail polish, silk stockings, and two dozen malted milk chocolate bars.

The ship's dining hall did not induce appetite. Its smell pervaded everything – a strange amalgam of steam kitchen, bad ventilation, uninspired cooking, and too many men. We carried our own utensils –"tools," they were called – and after meals washed them by dipping them into a filthy communal tub with some sort of strong disinfectant.

My chocolate bars were more appealing. I wolfed down five of them, deliberately forfeiting five nights of unspeakable passion. Then the *Aquitania* began a long deep roll and pitch in heavy seas. Three decks down, in the hot stinking clutter of humanity, my stomach and the chocolate bars abandoned ship.

For two or three days most of us were disgustingly seasick, dividing our miserable hours between the hammocks, the heads, and the rail. It was years before I could eat malted milk bars again and months before I could even face the leftovers in the bottom of my kit bag. By then they were squashed flat, fossilized, and melded with a hardened mass of red nail polish. Not one sex-starved British girl showed the slightest interest in them.

Steppler, the entrepreneur, got himself assigned to the ship's library. There he made friends with an air crew navigator who went on deck every day and took sightings with a sextant, to keep his hand in. Then, with a library atlas, he plotted our course which was supposed to be secret. We all knew we were traveling without an escort but Steppler found out we were taking evasive action: south of Halifax, then north again, and finally looping around the top of Ireland. Sometimes Allied planes picked us up but for two days we were on our own.

The rest of us, earnestly trying to keep down our lunch, did not dwell on any of this, which was just as well. Had we been torpedoed, and *if* we'd made it up from the lower decks, we wouldn't have lasted long in the icy Atlantic without other vessels to pick us up.

But the *Aquitania* steamed safely up the Firth of Clyde in six days. The hills of Greenock, Scotland, freshening with the first kiss of spring, closed around us. Britain! At last I was in the land of my ancestors and the hurricane's eye of the war.

We lined up at a cable desk to send home safe-arrival messages (reduced to a few stock phrases, so they could be easily codified). How my parents must have waited, waited, waited for my message through that anxious week. How they must have worried. But needlessly.

Midway through our voyage, the Allied forces under Montgomery began battling their way across the Rhine. Were we too late? Was there anything left for us to do?

Chapter Nine

From the beginning, England felt right. My father's family was here. The things he revered and believed in were here. The King and Winston Churchill were here. And here were the valiant people we admired and cheered on through the darkest years of war.

As our train sped down the length of the country I drank in its sights. Everything pleased me: immaculate hedgerows; stout brick walls with broken glass embedded along their tops, a kind of privacy that I endorsed; scrunched-together houses and smoke-stacks; cobblestones and village squares.

I thought of my father and how he would have reveled in these scenes—yet I could not place his distant figure, in World War I khaki and gleaming cavalry boots, in this setting. He had not steeped me in memories of England, simply because he couldn't recall them at will. He could not recount in glowing detail—as my mother could—long anecdotes from childhood. Something, everything, that happened to him in the trenches seemed to have blotted out all but random fragments of his prewar past.

Rather, what I saw here were pages from *Nicholas Nickleby*, *Chatterbox*, and *The Boy's Own Annual*. And echoes of Mister Adams and Auntie May, whose lives and accents epitomized to me the civility of England.

We detrained at Bournemouth on the south coast, to be billeted in hotels of faded elegance. They had no staffs or services—just damp, chilly, barren rooms with beds, communal toilets, and crumbling plaster—but were infinitely more romantic than Mont Joli's comfortable puke-green barracks. I dreamed of a day when I might return as a wealthy correspondent to a hotel like this, with morning tea served on a silver tray.

The blackout was still on. Train compartments still bore warning lists:

DURING BLACKOUT HOURS

1. KEEP ALL BLINDS DRAWN
2. KEEP ALL WINDOWS SHUT except when it is
   necessary to lower them so passengers may open
   the doors to alight.
3. MAKE CERTAIN the train is at the platform and
   that you alight on the platform side. . . .

The day we reached Bournemouth the last of Hitler's V-2 rockets fell on British soil (no one knew it *was* the last, of course). Below us on the Channel beaches, facing France where Hitler once had ranted and postured, concrete tank barriers and barbed wire were still strung along the sand. Munitions dumps loomed surprisingly behind hedges in quiet country lanes. *England*—champion of the Battle of Britain, survivor of the blitz, bastion of the Empire!

We took a two-week modified commando course, swinging over water on ropes, climbing cliffs and walls, crawling on our bellies, charging at dummies with bayonets, tossing grenades, and firing rifles and Sten guns. At our final rifle shoot we each tossed a shilling into a pot.

To everyone's amazement, I placed second among forty men. Sam Glassford's astonished "Nice shooting, Lad!" was worth more to me than the two quid which went to the man who beat me, a former bank clerk. Should I have been a killer instead of a mechanic? Probably not; the air force rated me a "first class" rifle shot but only second class with the Sten (when I fired it from the hip, one of two positions required, I sprayed bullets all over the target and into neighboring counties).

Our postings came through. Although we did not know it, the war in Europe was in its final month. The Russians had just captured Vienna; the Canadians in Holland had fought their way to the North Sea. But a few men were still needed on the continent for the Tactical Air Force. The best tradesmen (and the most enterprising) including Glassford and Steppler, went to TAF. The rest of us were sprinkled through Yorkshire, home of No. 6 RCAF Bomber Group.

No. 6 Group had fourteen squadrons at such mellifluous stations as Skipton-on-Swale, Linton-on-Ouse, East Moore, Topcliffe, Dishforth, Leeming, and Middleton St. George. My station, Wombleton, was nestled among farmers' fields in the picturesque Yorkshire dales, about fifteen miles from the market town of Thirsk, known to a later generation as James Herriot country.

Here, at last, I laid hands on a fighting plane, the almost-legendary bomber extolled in a thousand newscasts when I was still a farm boy: the incomparable Lancaster. The Lancs were scattered around the perimeter of the airfield in wartime fashion, each in its parking space with rickety flight shacks nearby. I walked around my first one, awed, like a mouse surveying an elephant. It stood twenty feet high. Its tires came up to my shoulder. Its wings, with the red-blue air force roundels on their tips, spanned 102 feet.

It was the most successful bomber of the war. Pilots claimed that, for its size and power, it handled almost like a fighter. Normally it carried 14,000 pounds of bombs and the "Specials" of the Dambuster Squadron had carried 22,000—more even than the Americans' gargantuan B-29 Superfortresses. When its four Merlin engines with their three-bladed props revved up, the ground trembled. I snapped photo after boring photo of Lancasters in total repose, to prove to myself and to the folks back home that these craft and I actually trod the same earth.

For two years No. 6 Group had pounded German targets on the continent. A month before our arrival Luftwaffe fighters had made a daring last-ditch foray into the heart of hated Bomber Group, shooting down a number of Lancs returning from Germany. Now operations were almost at a standstill. We maintained a daily schedule of sorts: out to the flight shack (labeled "Damn Seldom Inn" by some earlier wit); check the monster's metal skin, camouflaged in green and brown earth colors, for loose rivets; clamber sixty-nine feet from nose to tail, examining the bewildering array of wires and cables for fraying or undue slack; check the hydraulic system for leaks; check the mammoth tires for cuts and bruises.

We lived six or eight to a Nissen hut with palliasses (coarse pallets) for mattresses and bolsters for pillows. The Nissen was long and low with corrugated metal roof and sides that arched to the ground, like a giant's drainpipe cut lengthwise. With a coal stove in the middle, it was surprisingly snug.

We rolled up our pant cuffs—an unmilitary act that would have given Corporal Collins apoplexy—to escape the Yorkshire mud. For a quid or two, we bought bikes to commute to the flight shacks or into town. Life was as free as any of us had known since civvy street, and we rejoiced.

The revolving door of air force life had flung me into a new batch of strangers. Easygoing slow-talking Don Lindsay and his beloved pipe. Gruff Vern Harper with a George C. Scott profile. Eugene "Smitty" Smith with his square decent face and mid-West twang; although now an Edmontonian, he wore "U.S.A." on his RCAF shoulder patches, marking the land of his birth. Howie "Goodie" Goodyear, short and perky with a pale skinny face abrim with deviltry. "Red" Langley and "Mac" MacLean; I never knew their real first names but wished for a nickname, too.

Mac was one of many Toronto friends. My rural gaucherie and the invisible line between "city" and "country" were gone. City boys never ceased to rib me about a home town with the improbable name of "Shamrock" but it was done by rote, and we all rather enjoyed it. We were equals at last.

Ours was the special intimacy of men in groups. We knew more of one another—our habits, quirks, and secret worries—than parents, wives, or sweethearts ever did. I knew a man who hated to bare his back because of its thick pelt of hair. Another wore gloves almost everywhere because he was embarrassed by warts on his hands. A third told me in deepest confidence that he was a virgin, saving himself for marriage—such old-fashioned morality in the war's free-sex environment that he dared not reveal it to the Nissen hut gang.

Our jobs were "a piece of cake" except when somebody "pranged" a "kite" and made it "u/s," which really "brassed us off." (Translation: the job was easy unless someone cracked up an aircraft, making it unserviceable, which exasperated us mechanics because it meant more work.) We were always "binding" about something. Good weather was a bind, if you hated work. Keen "types" or "bods" liked "bags of" flying. The rest of us liked to get off early and go to York, a "wizard" place for girls.

Mess hall food was a bind. Our palates were not attuned to the flat taste of powdered eggs or the chalky flavor of powdered milk. And one more serving of mutton, we swore, and we'd "baaaa" on roll call. But farmers around us gladly bartered produce for Canadian cigarettes (ambrosia compared to their own rank Wild Woodbines) so at night we feasted on fresh eggs fried in our mess tins over the coal stove.

Our egg dealer was Young Albert (pronounced "Yungh Ahl-but," from the Stanley Holloway monologue "Albert & the Lion"). This loutish farm youth, with the street smarts of an alley cat, had the classic Yorkshire tongue: he actually said "Eeee, bah Gum!" Bursting with self-importance at mingling with the military, Young Albert told boring dirty jokes that dwelt on barn-yard sexual functions.

Sometimes our tame Italian, a swarthy peaceable prisoner of war, stopped in after his local farm labor. Italian soldiers were deemed harmless as kittens; this one was allowed to run free at night as long as he got back before bedtime. White teeth spar-kling through his permanent five o'clock shadow, he bummed cigarettes and tried to sell us hand-tooled cigarette cases and ashtrays, fashioned from scrounged metal. His specialty showed a thoroughly proper Edwardian lady and gent on the top of an ashtray; on the underside, they were doing obscene things.

We discovered the magic of British pubs. No more Presbyterian guilt. No more sordid Canadian beer parlors where men and women in segregated rooms sat hunched around beer-spattered tables bent on one objective—getting drunk. Here was a commu-nity center of light and warmth where young and old nursed pints together all evening with no surly waiters goading them to buy more. We tossed darts, shuffled dominoes, and sang at the top of our lungs over the piano. We leaned against the bar—our pom-padours Brylcreemed in glossy billows, our caps tucked into our battle dress shoulder straps—and furtively checked the mirror to see if girls behind us were admiring our blue backs and perfect bums.

The English tolerantly (for the most part) let us monopolize their hallowed locals, taught us the ways of civilized drinking, and became our friends. We swelled their cash registers and—when the publican called "Time, gentlemen, please!"—teetered home on our bikes along black country roads. Sometimes we paused to be sick, having misjudged the potence of six pints of bitter or two of Guinness Ale.

> Under the spreading chestnut tree
> A glass of Guinness stood.
> The smith, a mightier man is he—
> His Guinness did him good.
> And would it do the same for me?
> My Guinness, yes it would!
> English billboard, 1940s

The pubs, the billboards, the ads for Bisto and Brylcreem, were part of England's potpourri that summer. Things like Jane of *The Daily Mirror*, reigning queen of the British comic strips, who every day managed to get out of her clothes with a discreet flash of breast or thigh, risqué fare in that pre-porn era.

Things like tea, dished up in hundreds of service centers all over the land. They were our homes away from home and our uniforms were tickets of entry. The centers—some operated by the Sally Ann or Legion or YMCA or Britain's Navy, Army and Air Force Institute (NAAFI), some by independent groups—ran day and night. The women volunteers who ran them, unsung heroines of the war, were unfailingly kind. They chatted us up when we were lonely, gave directions when we were lost, played cards with us, sewed buttons on our shirts, helped buy gifts for our mothers and sweethearts. They fed us good home-cooked meals for twenty-five cents and plied us with tea.

Fortress England floated on an ocean of tea, insipid-looking stuff, pale from too much condensed milk, yet somehow comforting. Tea served from NAAFI trucks on tarmacs and in hangars. "Tea up!" The clarion call brought us on the double with our tin mugs. Tea in servicemen's canteens wherever we went on leave. Tea from stalls in the soft murky light of yet another railway station.

In one such station I waited with my tea for a train back to Wombleton when a load of German prisoners pulled in. A blond young soldier leaned out a coach window, hair tumbled on his forehead. Our eyes met and locked, in stares of mutual disdain. Full of swagger, I wrote to my father:

April 21, 1945

They were all young, cocky, arrogant kids in their late 'teens, well fed and apparently quite healthy, riding in comfortable railway cars. Those boys haven't had enough war yet.

It never occurred to me that I could be describing myself.

A packet of snapshots from Belsen concentration camp found its way among us. It was difficult to comprehend those emaciated bodies, and those skeletons. Had these been men, women, children? Had all this happened a mere few hundred miles away? How could humans do this to other humans?

April 29, 1945

They are certainly the most horrible sights that a decent person could bear to see. I think it has struck home to most of our people but I doubt if it has been properly drummed into the Germans yet.

My crippling self-consciousness was melting away. My father's admonition that "little boys should be seen and not heard" was bad advice for adulthood, I realized. (Anyway, he'd never heeded it himself.) The very act of crossing the ocean had changed me. Here, we were liked, even loved, for our uniforms. I was learning to enjoy the thrilling wartime undercurrent of do-it-now-tomorrow-may-be-too-late—totally contrary to my Depression-era caution.

Among us in Britain was a pecking order. At the top were the Yanks, favored by many British women and hated by most other men. The only thing wrong with Yanks, we said, was that they were "overpaid, oversexed, and over here." They had the most money, the best-tailored uniforms, and, like so many Americans *en masse*, were noisy, arrogant, and patronizing to those unfortunate mortals who had not been born American.

Fortunately, many right-minded British girls found us Canadians almost as appealing. I felt sorry for the British military (although we derisively referred to them as "pongos," a disparaging name originally applied to an African ape). They suffered here from the same blight we'd known in Canada: familiarity.

Not that I was an instant Don Juan. A stunning black-haired maiden named Josie dumped me after one date in Bournemouth. One Saturday I traveled 130 miles from Wombleton to Blackpool, to rendezvous with a girl I'd met the weekend before. She stood me up, I missed the last train home, and the city was packed, so I spent the night on a railway station bench—short sections with wooden arms between. I slept under my plastic raincoat with my feet in one section, my body in the next and my head braced against a wooden arm, and returned to camp shaped like an accordion.

But there were happier times with Land Army girls, British WDs, big-breasted girls from York with beer on their sweet lips, and a doe-eyed beauty named Paula whose favorite epithet for all things was "Eeh, that's *smashing!*", in a Yorkshire accent thick as treacle.

We latecomers were reaping the gratitude that earlier Canadians had earned. One spring afternoon two elderly ladies—miniatures of Auntie May Walker, as fragile and elegant as Spode teacups—accosted me as I left the Wombleton train.

"We just want to thank you boys for coming over here and helping us beat Hitler," said one, eyes bright and birdlike behind her spectacles. On behalf of the Dominion of Canada and its armed forces, I accepted their thanks and thanked *them* for Britain's kindness to us.

Hitler was more than beaten; on May 1 the Germans officially announced that he was dead. Three days later I got a week's leave to visit assorted English Collinses in and around London. We knew victory was near but I never dreamed I would celebrate it in the most appropriate place on earth.

I reached the great city at 3 A.M. and hung around a service center near King's Cross station until the underground opened. In the morning, the Shamrock kid wended his way through the heart of London.

May 13, 1945

I crossed the central part of the city by tube. Mr. Adams was quite right; it certainly is a grand system and though I had two changes on the way I made it through without getting lost. And so I wound up at Victoria station in South London to catch the noon train to Faversham. . . .

Aunt Kitty was waiting—she who had written us letters all through my boyhood, never failing to send a monogrammed handkerchief on my birthday. She who wrote also to Uncle Ted Collins in Australia and Uncle George in northern Saskatchewan, her letters the threads that bound us all to England. She was short, in her seventies, with my father's red hair, blue eyes, and unquenchable spirit. We bussed to Dunkirk, the Kentish village where she lived with a friend in a four-room cottage among orchards and flowers.

Now my English roots began to reach around me. That night she brought out a family treasure: my grandfather Samuel Collins' silver pocket watch with a snap cover and a tiny compass at the end of the chain. Grandfather had died many years before.

"This is for your father," she said. "I never dared send it through the mails. You shall take it back to him, when you go home some day."

In the morning, after serving my tea in bed, she took me back to London to show off Jack's boy from Canada to the clan. They greeted me like royalty: Uncle George Tye, a London postman, a gaunt kind little man, and Aunt Edie, she too with the Collins hair and eyes. And daughter Betty, and young George and his wife, Jessie. Son Jack had been lost three years before, after six weeks at sea with the Merchant Navy. Aunt Edie still grew teary eyed at his memory.

In their scrap of back yard I crawled down their rabbit hole of an air raid shelter—corrugated iron covered with earth, boarded and bricked up inside. It was only six feet by six, and five feet high, but five people and the cat had slept there every night for six months during the worst of the blitz. Their house had been hit, but not seriously.

Cousin Billy Dobinson had been bombed too; and cousin Sam Collins, his beautiful blonde wife, Margaret, their cat, and their swearing parrot, Polly, had lost their London home to the bombs. These people—*my own kin, my own blood!*—were the same durable Britons we had read about, heard about, saluted from our farmhouse through the war. And so matter-of-fact about it all.

Sam and Margaret's wartime story was typical: London's story in microcosm. Both were trained as air raid wardens and Sam was in the Home Guard. Like most Londoners they also held full-time jobs in the city—Margaret in Woolwich Arsenal, which the Germans yearned to obliterate, but did not—and at night hoped they'd live through the blitz and maybe even get a decent sleep.

One June night in 1944, they and the cat were squeezed into their tiny back-yard shelter, while Polly stayed in the house, his cage bundled in a heavy chenille curtain. Suddenly the skies were full of Hitler's newest terror: "doodlebugs," robot V-1 flying bombs. Margaret came to fear them even more than the more lethal V-2 guided missiles that rained on London months later. The doodlebugs buzzed over with a horrible chatter, then cut out. The sudden unnerving silence meant they were coming down—somewhere near.

That night one of them nosed into Sam and Margaret's street, killing nine people and injuring many more a few yards away. The concussion blew Sam against the end of the shelter and knocked him out. When he revived, debris still tumbling on their tin roof, he had to restrain Margaret who was wailing, "We *must* get Polly!"

In a few minutes the dust cleared and they picked their way up into the yard. The house was a ruin.

"Polly, Polly, where are you?" cried Margaret, over and over. Finally, out of the rubble, a small squawky voice answered, " 'Allo, dear!"

Polly moved in with friends while Sam and Margaret lived in the shelter for six months, well into the V-2 raids. The day I met them, they were cheerfully toughing it out in a temporary cottage at Southend-by-Sea.

The Collins relatives fulfilled all my preconceptions, and enhanced my love affair with England. One night, as I walked to a corner shop with cousin Fred Carrell, husband of Winnie Collins, piano music wafted from an upstairs window. Fred—an ordinary bloke with some ordinary job, but a classical music-lover—cocked an ear.

"Is that Chopin?" he said courteously, as if *I* might know. It was something Mister Adams would have said. *Ah yes,* I thought, *civility and culture have been rubbed into them through the ages.*

Aunt Kitty led me around the city by double-decker bus. Now my father's London rose up around me. We rode the free ferry across the Thames. "Be sure to tell Jack you did this," Aunt Kitty said, "because he did too." We saw the riverside pub where another uncle had drowned. (He had been fond of the grape and may have fallen in drunk.) We saw where Grandfather Collins' bakeshop stood for twenty-five years; the Tyes produced the inscribed clock he'd won in a cake-baking contest. Once Aunt Kitty said, with misty eyes, "When your dad and your Uncle George came back over here from Canada in the winter of 1914, oh, the times we had, singing and laughing, before they went to the front!" Suddenly I saw him vividly—slim, straight backed and devil-may-care, before the trenches did him in.

On the evening of May 7 came the announcement: tomorrow was V-E Day. Victory in Europe! The day we had prayed and waited for since 1939. Instantly the celebrations began. At 11 P.M. a party rollicked out of the corner pub, singing past the Tyes' home in Plumstead. I recorded it for my father:

May 13, 1945

> They touched on everything from "Mother Ireland" to "Land of Hope and Glory" complete with trills and harmony as of a fifteen-piece orchestra. The sky was full of fireworks and the light of bonfires, and all the searchlights were weaving around the sky making lovely patterns. On the Thames, the fog horns and tooters were piping out the "V" signal in Morse Code. . . .

On V-E Day we went down to the city. From Nelson's Monument in Trafalgar Square we wended our way along Whitehall. It was a day such as London had never seen before nor will again. The sidewalks had vanished: we moved through canyons of rejoicing people. Windowsills, balustrades, lamp posts were draped with small boys, office girls, men and women in every uniform of the Commonwealth and its allies. Strangers sang and danced together and locked in passionate kisses. Anything was permissible on V-E Day. I looked on wistfully, from within a decorous island of cousins and aunts.

We push past No. 10 Downing Street, where a London bobby stands on guard. Everywhere, there is an enormous muffled din, the sound of a million hoarse voices waiting for something else to cheer. We move along Westminster Bridge and there are the spires of Parliament, and Big Ben bathed in batteries of floodlights. *Yes, yes, just as I knew they'd look, from the newsreels!* Into Westminster Abbey, thronged with sightseers like us, and others kneeling to silently thank their God that the war is over. I gape up at the stained glass windows that survived the blitz, and down at the tombs of famous men. *I am in the Abbey!*

We pause for lunch—a plate of borsch in a Russian tea-room, of all things—then up Regent Street to the BBC building, the link between Britain and our farmhouse all through the war. Later I will describe it painstakingly for my parents: "a handsome modern-looking building, all streamlined and painted white."

Across Piccadilly and up The Mall to Buckingham Palace. *How my dad would love to be here!* The crowds have been waiting, waiting for hours. The excitement is close to frenzy. A center balcony is draped in red and gold ("otherwise the Palace is quite ordinary looking, and needs a new coat of paint," reports our practical correspondent from Shamrock). "The King and Queen will be coming out soon!" someone tells us. "And the princesses! And Winston!" And for me, this is *the* great moment of the war, so far.

Above all, I longed to see Churchill. For five years his growling presence had dominated our lives. On the farm we feasted on each scrap of trivia: that he favored bow ties, a high stiff hat, huge Havana cigars, and snifters of brandy. We chuckled together upon hearing that Bernard Montgomery, Britain's feisty general, once primly claimed one hundred–percent efficiency because he neither smoked nor drank, and Churchill shot back, "I use both and my efficiency is two hundred percent!" Even my teetotaling mother laughed at that.

World War II had tested all his eloquence, courage, stubbornness, and patriotism. Through the blackest moments he lashed us on with his unforgettable voice, vibrant, defiant, now soaring like an actor's, now sonorous like a churchman's.

Now this was Winston's day.

But now—oh wretched fate!—Aunt Kitty's ancient legs gave out. With a sinking heart I heard one of the cousins say, "Want to go 'ome, then, luv?"

As a dutiful nephew, but with many a yearning backward glance, I joined the family convoy piloting her through the ocean of humanity back to the Tyes' small brick house. There we celebrated mildly with ale and pranced around the parlor to a few choruses of "Knees Up Mother Brown." Aunt Kitty, making a phenomenal recovery, joined in.

I never saw the grand Old Man. That afternoon he spoke on the BBC. At 5:30 he stepped out on a Buckingham Palace balcony with the King and Queen, waved his famous cigar, and flashed his V-for-Victory sign. About 6 P.M. he appeared on a flag-draped balcony of the Ministry of Health building in Whitehall, and his voice trumpeted over loudspeakers to the adoring throngs.

"This is your victory! . . ." he told them.

As the cheers welled up around him like a tidal wave he thundered one more time, "Were we downhearted?"

"No!" the crowds roared back one more time.

And then the war in Europe was officially over.

Chapter Ten

After the V-E Day binge came the emotional hangover. For the British people there were still queues, rationing, frayed clothing, worn-out buses and trains, not enough cars or housing. Privation was tolerable in war — it had even helped stiffen their resolve — but not in peace. In the July general election, a disgruntled public threw out their hero and mine, Churchill, in favor of the Labor party. I was stunned and indignant. A true son of Jack Collins, I loathed socialism. And what a dirty deal for Winston! But, of course, I hadn't gone without necessities for five hard years.

For me, V-E Day brought limbo. I was glad the war in Europe was over, even though I'd done so little. But what next? Long-service troops would go home but we newcomers could forget about that. Some of us might go to the Pacific where the Japanese war seemed far from over. Some might yet go to the Continent. Some might stay in England and help wind down air bases. We waited, and filled the idle days with small events.

June 16, 1945

Down at the hangar I don't have a job — it's more what you might call a "position." We have a few kites to look after but as they don't fly there isn't any work. Every other afternoon is free, plus one day off during the week and usually the weekend. . . . Young Albert was in the other evening. Most of the boys were out but we made a few deals. I sold him two packages of cigarettes (which I won at bingo) for four bob. Seeing as that is about fifty cents apiece I guess I didn't lose much.

On the streets, children still hailed us with the wartime catch phrase "Any gum, chum?" (in Yorkshire it came out "guhm, chuhm"). We grinned and doled out Doublemint or Lifesavers from our endless supply. In our local pub an acquaintance named Charlie, a gregarious well-dressed civilian in his late thirties, became uncommonly eager to chat me up and buy rounds of bitter. It turned out he wanted a favor.

"Could you get me a box of chocolates and some nice stockings for me old mum?" he begged. "Mum" was probably a bleached blonde of nineteen, but I finally got a box of candy from Canada. Unfortunately, it was rather thin, and battered by the mails. Charlie stopped buying rounds.

A local farmer took us crow hunting. We didn't hit any, which pleased me, but it was good to be walking in fields again. Sometimes we biked for hours through the Yorkshire countryside. The roads were almost traffic free—gasoline was still scarce for civilians (although we routinely cleaned our uniforms in aviation gas). We soared like hawks through sunny flower-scented dales, stopping for lunches and beers at wayside pubs. Once we found a gang of small boys playing rounders—something like baseball—on a village green, so we joined them, to our mutual delight.

My worldly new self knew of a hideaway restaurant in Boroughbridge, about twenty-five miles from Wombleton, that had limited supplies of such luxuries as steaks and eggs. One Sunday I led four friends there. We devoured a "lovely" dinner of grilled chicken, chips, and "real eggs" (as I wrote home). The bill for five totalled a pound (about five dollars). In high good humor we began shuffling it from man to man to see who'd get stuck with it. A middle-aged English couple at the next table smiled indulgently. Suddenly "the old chap," as I later described him— he was probably about forty-five—sprang up and seized our bill.

We stared at him and one another, speechless. Then one of us blurted, in some embarrassment, "Sorry sir, we're not really broke. Just clowning around."

"No, do let me pay it," he insisted. "Our son trained with the RAF in Canada and you Canucks treated him with such kindness. We're so glad to repay the favor in this a small way." We lingered, talking to them, for a half-hour.

My boyhood friend, Roy Bien—whose presence in the RCAF had drawn me in behind him—was stationed only thirty-five miles north at Thornaby near the coast. He'd been a wireless air gunner on Air Sea Rescue with an RAF squadron since midwar and would soon go home with his English war bride. One evening we went to dinner, he wearing the optional wedge cap instead of his flat hat, so the sight of a pilot officer fraternizing with an erk would not give senior officers heartburn.

There was no barrier of rank. The years swiftly melted as we talked about home, and our hopes for the future. He ordered wine and I thought, *How sophisticated we Shamrock boys have become!* Back home, wine was hideous plonk in fifty-cent bottles, guzzled in alleys by old derelicts.

Bill Steppler, ever in the forefront, wrote that he was going home from the Continent to train for service in the Pacific. On the back of a snapshot he scribbled, " 'Till our ways meet or all Hell freezes over, Your nomadic partner in crimes." *Would* our paths cross again? I waited. I worked at my Newspaper Institute of America lessons, in fits and starts, and signed up for an RCAF educational course on business.

July 13, 1945

> Today the instructor had each member of the class get up and introduce himself and tell a little of his past history. As we were all strangers to one another it was good experience. . . . Yester-day a man gave an hour's talk on salesmanship. That was very interesting.

"Very interesting." This from a youth who, two years ago, could barely stammer out his name in public! The fact that I spoke before a roomful of strangers showed how far I'd come in two years.

But I was not quite ready for the stage. A slick-talking airman, who wore "U.S.A." on his shoulder patches and said he'd worked in Hollywood, tried to organize a talent show. Smitty and I offered "If You Wore a Tulip" and "I Want a Girl, Just Like the Girl . . .", making up in volume what we lacked in harmony. The man from Hollywood listened, noncommittally, with a tight smile. We left crestfallen. In the Nissen hut we'd received rather good reviews for our rendition of "My brother's a poor missionary . . ." The show never got off the ground.

On a long weekend in Edinburgh a helpful woman in a service center asked if I wanted a city tour.

"I'd like to see a newspaper office."

She stared at me as though I'd gone mad.

"I'll see what I can do."

A morning later, with three civilians, I prowled through the editorial offices and print shop of *The Scotsman*. An elderly reporter stared at me quizzically and inquired in an oatmeal-porridge accent, "Why're ye no out drinkin' beer wi' yer mates, laddie?" I smiled enigmatically, breathed deep the heady smell of newsprint, and went away clutching my name set in a slug of metal type.

At the end of July Smitty, Red, Mac, Goodie, and I struck out for seven days' leave in northern Ireland. On the evening train to the west coast, to catch a boat across the Irish Sea, a British Wren took the last empty seat in our compartment, beside me. She was pretty and flirtatious. She flirted with *me*. The bold new me flirted right back. Someone—it would have been Mac or Goodie—thoughtfully unscrewed the light bulb in the compartment. It was not the ideal setting for romance, with four sniggering friends practically on my lap, but one did one's best in wartime.

Coming up for air between kisses, I asked rhetorically, "Are you married?"

"Yes, a bit."

"A *bit!* Where's your husband?"

"Away. In the army. Overseas."

"Oh. That's too bad."

"Too bad for him," she said saucily.

She got off at Preston. I joined her on the platform to say good-bye. "Sure you don't want to get off here too?" she said. It was tempting. My puritan defences were almost down. But we were all booked for Ireland and . . . and I didn't *quite* have the nerve. Still, to my cohorts on the train, my stature had soared to five, on a scale of ten.

"Collins!" cried Goodyear, when I returned. "You old Casanova!" He savored his turn of phrase. "Casanova . . . Cass Collins!" From then on I was Cass to him, MacLean, and a few others. At last I had a nickname like everybody else.

The next morning we checked into a Canadian Legion hostel in Belfast. As so often during the war, the Legion was the best address in town for a serviceman. I felt a deep affinity for this city that my father claimed as his birthplace. Somewhere here were graves of ancestors and probably some living, albeit distant, kin. A Legion lady told me that a Collins was one of Ireland's national heroes. "So I sez to the lady, I sez, 'that's us all right!' ", I wrote my father.

Although Belfast was not particularly scenic, the pubs opened at 10 A.M., so we pronounced it a civilized place. But we were not just pub-crawlers. One sunny morning we climbed a hill high above the city and took pictures. We traveled to Londonderry and trudged the Giant's Causeway, a natural formation of six-sided stone pillars.

All through that day a near-forgotten tune played softly in my head. I was fourteen, trembling on the stage of Shamrock's community hall, scratching out the melody on my violin while my mentor, Mister Adams, accompanied me on piano. They gave me first prize in the category (there was only one other violinist) – a small bronze medal that read "Athletic Championship Sask Schools." It *had* been a sort of musical marathon but Mister Adams, with consummate skill, kept up with me over the finish line. And now that tune, "Danny Boy" – or "Londonderry Air" to give it its proper name – surged up from my memory on this Irish stone pile.

Smitty and I went to a dance. As I scanned the scene, and the band broke into "Sentimental Journey," a new hit from North America, I saw a girl on the sidelines. It sounds impossibly romantic now, but I knew instantly that she was special.

She was chestnut haired, slim and softly rounded, just verging into womanhood. Her eyes – dark brown, demure but full of lurking humor – and the rich curve of her mouth caught me first. She stood alone, but composed; clearly she had no fear of being a wallflower. I crossed the floor like a shot.

"Would you like to dance?"

She looked up, and the smile was everything the eyes had promised.

"Why, yes," she said, in the Irish lilt that turned Bel*fast* into Bel*fast*. She danced well, meaning she could follow me around the floor without getting stepped on.

We talked as though we'd known each other a lifetime. Her name was Constance Macnab. Her parents were transplanted Scots but she was a sure-enough Belfast girl. She was seventeen, only three years younger than I, and a comptometer (adding machine) operator in a downtown office. She lived with her parents and had come to the dance with an older girlfriend, Sheelagh, and the latter's man, Gwyn, a civilian of about forty, whose worldly-wise eyes examined me with mild amusement.

Connie said she didn't have a steady boyfriend. There *was* a U.S. army officer, also named Bob, also stationed in the British Isles, also smitten by her, but there was nothing definite between them. And yes, she had a ride home with Gwyn and Sheelagh but, yes, I could call her tomorrow. I went back to the Legion hostel with wings on my size nine boots.

The next day about noon, the kindly ladies at the front desk said there was a visitor. It was Connie Macnab. She'd just dropped by on her lunch hour to say hello and . . . And Howie Goodyear's eyes bulged.

"Cass! *Cass! Another* one? What's her name? Where'd you find *her?*"

From then on we did everything together: horseback riding, ice skating on an artificial rink, movies, dances. I saw little of my companions, except when Connie was at work, or late at night, when they tried to pump me on my progress. I held them at bay; too much comradely nosiness could spoil this, and everything about this girl was right.

I liked the way she dressed, in soft cashmere sweaters, tailored slacks, tartan skirts, on special occasions a tweedy suit. Her sense of humor meshed with mine. I even took up smoking, because Connie smoked. I hated the taste and never inhaled, but the *style* of it appealed to me—the perfect white cylinder plucked from its pack, her hands cupped around mine as we lit up, the studied nonchalance of flicking the ash. It gave us one more thing in common.

She invited me home for dinner. It was a brick house in a pleasant residential block on Antrim Road. The Macnabs were solidly mid-upper class. I took along the ration tickets that servicemen were issued on leave, the best gift we could offer a British hostess in those years. Her mother, warm and wise, had bequeathed her charm to Connie. Her young brother and sister were impish. Her father, who was "in textiles," was courteous but formal. He always called his daughter "Constance," which rolled stiffly from his tongue and made her giggle behind his back. He regarded me with veiled suspicion, as any father of a nubile daughter should. I was excruciatingly respectful and polite.

On my last night in Ireland we went to dinner at Sheelagh's home, a handsome place far from the center of Belfast, where she was more or less in residence with Gwyn. As the evening grew late, I was invited to stay over. Connie already had an overnight pass from home.

We were given separate bedrooms, but we clung together until dawn. When I left, she slipped from her middle finger a small silver ring with a woven-knot design. "A friendship ring," she called it, fitting it on my small finger. I read much more into it. Nothing else was said but I knew Connie Macnab was the girl I wanted to marry.

Only a keenly perceptive parent could have read such momentous news between the lines of a note I scribbled home during the Irish sea crossing.

August 6, 1945

I had a wonderful leave. I met a very nice girl and family and they were swell to me. The boys and I also went sightseeing one day near Londonderry. All in all, I'd like to go again.

On the train back to Wombleton, the strains of "Sentimental Journey" still running through my head, I picked up the London *Times*. It was August 7. I flipped past the front page of classified ads to page four, where world news habitually appeared. A two-column headline read:

FIRST ATOMIC BOMB HITS JAPAN
EXPLOSION EQUAL TO 20,000 TONS OF TNT

American President Harry Truman had announced this incredible bomb the previous day. It had harnessed, the stories said, "the basic power of the universe." It had wreaked havoc on a Japanese city called Hiroshima.

It took another bomb on Nagasaki, on August 9, and a fuller report on the devastation, for me to faintly grasp what it meant. Even then I, like most other ordinary people, had no real understanding of the horror that had been unleashed in those two days.

The Japanese, we knew, had committed atrocities against civilians and military prisoners of war. Now they had been suddenly, awesomely crushed. Years later, reading John Hersey's *Hiroshima*, I would fully understand but now, two days after the Japanese Empire surrendered, my reaction was perhaps typical of many on our side: the enemy got what they deserved.

August 16, 1945

Well, it's over! So much has happened since I last wrote that I hardly know where to begin. But of course, V-J Day is the big news, that and the atom bombs. It all happened in such rapid fire fashion that I don't know what to make of it all. I think, though, that we were, as usual, too soft with the Japs. The atom bomb may be inhuman but I guess we wouldn't feel guilty after what the Japs have done. A few more of those bombs and they wouldn't have stalled their reply [to the demand for surrender].

I also see by the paper that the British Empire is not accepting any responsibility for using the bomb. I think that is also darn foolish. We've got it now, for better or worse, and we'll never be able to hide it. We can just hope to God there won't be another war in our time.

But it's over anyway. It'll be a great day for China and all the fellows in the Far East. I don't know how it will affect us. The station was about to be cleared out and then the postings were all canceled. . . .

I sent a long affectionate letter to Connie Macnab but she didn't reply. Well, she'd *said* she wasn't a good letter-writer. . . . I swallowed my disappointment.

Soon it was pushed into the background. In less than a month I was on my way to Germany.

Chapter Eleven

It was four days of hurry-up-and-wait from Dover to Hamburg by Channel boat and slow trains – and a mental leap of six years. I was going into Hitler's Germany. Since 1939 I had actively hated the Germans. They were our mortal enemies. Their armies had crushed Poland, Czechoslovakia, Holland, Belgium, France. Their air force had showered death on London and Coventry. Their Gestapo had terrorized all of Europe. Their death camps had methodically tried to exterminate the Jews while the rest of the nation turned a blind eye.

Now I was going to live among them. We were not warriors, but we wore victors' uniforms. How should we behave? We had inherited the upper hand. How would it feel? Early in the war, Churchill had said, "The Germans are either at your throat or at your feet." Would they hate us or lick our boots? We each carried a rifle or Sten, and clips of ammunition. Would we need them?

I was jubilant. At last, a *real* adventure: the British Air Force of Occupation (BAFO)! This made up for all the listless months behind. Occupation was one thing that thousands of other servicemen had not done before me.

We landed at Ostende on the Belgian coast, moved to Blankenberge, and waited for a train. We took one another's pictures in a shopkeeper's doorway, grinning like kids let out of school: Mac MacLean, burly and bespectacled; an airman called "Duke"; and a new friend Al Heaton, whom I'd have hated for his matinee-idol good looks if he hadn't been such a nice guy. Everyone bought souvenir lapel pins, tiny daggers with mother-of-pearl handle and chrome-plated blade.

Finally the leather-lunged NCOs herded, coaxed, and bullied

us onto a train–"AWRIGHT YOU MEN, FALL IN"–bellowing names in alphabetical order for the inevitable roll call. Each time we moved in groups throughout those years, there was a roll call to round up strays. Whole wartime friendships were built around roll call: I might never have met Al Cooper if "Cooper" hadn't stood next to "Collins."

The train labored across Belgium into western Germany and crept over the Rhine at Wesel, on a temporary bridge flung up by engineers after Montgomery's 21st Army had fought across the river six months before. Beside us lay footprints of war: two other bridges, demolished by the retreating Nazis, crumpled and broken in the water.

The trip across Germany was even slower. The railways were overtaxed and decrepit. From the train windows at Hannover I shot pictures of a bomb-ruined cityscape in pale October sun. We traveled most of the last day without food and, at one interminable stop in the middle of nowhere, roamed into the autumn fields to pick green apples. Finally we reached Hamburg, seventy-five miles inland from the North Sea, on the Elbe River. Nothing had prepared us for that sight.

I knew, from newspaper reports and from idle chitchat on this four-day journey, that we were going into the worst-bombed city in Europe. Hamburg had been Germany's greatest seaport and shipbuilding center, and a major submarine base. In July and August 1943, Bomber Command set out to crush it, to neutralize its output and to demoralize Hitler's empire.

Masses of bombers, from our very own Yorkshire dales, turned nine square miles of Hamburg into a sea of flame. In places the temperature rose to eighteen hundred degrees Fahrenheit. There were fire "blizzards"–hot winds surging at twice the force of a hurricane. Children were plucked from their parents' arms and sucked into the fire. People in unsealed shelters, though untouched by bombs, died from inhaling the scorching air. For six weeks Hamburg burned and smoldered. Now, two years later, we saw the aftermath.

The scene, slowly unreeling beside us as the train chugs in, almost defies belief. Hamburg is *still* shattered. I have come half expecting another London; the Collins relatives showed me streets with missing houses, neighborhoods with bombed-out blocks, rather like a mouth with missing teeth. London has cleaned up much of the mess. But here, as I stare into a city illuminated by faint moonlight and scanty street light, the rubble lies in mountains. This is not just bombing. This is devastation!

Overhead in the station, hundreds of square feet of windows are smashed; their frames stand out like bare bones. We hang out the windows, aghast, yet with a certain patriotic exultation. "Holy Christ, can you believe this?" murmurs the man beside me. I can't. I mutter something incoherent. I feel a tangle of emotions. On the one hand: *We really stuck it to the Nazis this time!* But then, *There were women and kids in there. . . .*

There was no more time to view the wreckage. We trucked twenty miles north-west to Uetersen, a former Luftwaffe base, now RCAF 126 Wing, the home of Spitfire fighter squadrons 411, 412, 416, and 443. The next morning I went to work with 6443 Service Echelon, attached to 443, the Hornet Squadron. Its motto was "Our sting is death." Its pilots had won a Distinguished Flying Order and six Distinguished Flying Crosses. One of the latter belonged to our current CO, Squadron Leader Cal Bricker. With our arrival, 443 had twenty-four pilots and ninety-five ground crew, with eighteen Mark XVI Spitfires.

Spitfire! The name rang like an ancient battle cry; my blood tingled at the sound of it. After the Battle of Britain every red-blooded boy of my generation worshipped the Spit. Lean and racy—thirty feet long, eleven feet high, with a low-wingspan of thirty-seven feet—it seemed poised as though about to soar, even when silent on the tarmac. In the air it could climb to forty thousand feet and its Rolls Royce engine could push it well over four hundred miles per hour—blinding speed in those times.

I felt wonderfully privileged to be working on Spitfires, even though the war was over and it didn't really count. Each of us was permanently assigned to one. Mine was 21X. I snapped pictures of it from every angle, fattening my famous album of motionless aircraft.

Our job was not overly demanding. The Wing was here to show the flag. Our Spitfires in the sky reminded the Russians, twenty-five miles away, that the British Zone was fully manned. It also helped the Jerries (we never called them Krauts or Huns) remember who were their new masters.

As soon as we solved the workings of the station—*How long do we work? What time do we eat? Where's the wet canteen? What kinda bad-asses have we got for NCOs? When do we get a pass into town?—*

essential "gen" on each new posting, we began visiting Hamburg on evenings or weekends, riding the backs of air force trucks or hitching lifts in passing Jeeps.

Officially we were forbidden to fraternize, a loose term that covered everything from dealing on the black market to visiting a German home or sleeping with a German girl. Until we got the lay of the land, we newcomers carefully avoided all but casual contacts with the Jerries, keeping eyes in the backs of our heads for SPs or the thoroughly nasty British Army MPs.

But there was no ban on viewing the city. The military had just lifted an order requiring us to carry our rifles into Hamburg. Certainly there was no need for them. We were in no danger of being mugged unless we wandered alone into certain rough districts that were designated out of bounds. The people were too preoccupied with survival. Hamburg was an eerie monument to the ugliness of war and the misery of defeat.

Sometimes I walked alone with a camera through silent avenues of rubble, meeting an occasional figure muffled against the chill, hurrying past with downcast eyes. All around me were vignettes of war: A fragment of shattered building, bolt upright like a shard of glass. An apartment block sliced vertically, its tiers of shattered rooms open to the leaden sky. The frame of a doorway, silhouetted against the dust and broken masonry that was once a home. An old woman, in heavy bib apron and head scarf, foraging for firewood. A solitary child squatting like a small watchful animal among ruins: he probably lived in a nearby cellar. Always, the brackish sickening smell of the debris. Corpses, they said, were still buried there.

Yet a dozen blocks away, in utter contrast, Hamburg showed a face of greed and need. In a crowded park nearer the city center, a feverish black market flourished day and night. The market was everywhere, of course. At Uetersen the barracks janitors, men of indeterminate age, all known as "The Jerry," would get you almost anything for cigarettes. Outside the Canada Club in downtown Hamburg — once the Phönix Hotel, now an RCAF recreation center — men and women shuffled back and forth with cameras and watches under their coats, a bit risky because the black market was *verboten*.

But in the park, although we all kept an eye open for cops, the barter was wide-open. SPs, MPs, and civilian police made only token efforts to enforce the law. Without the black market, many Germans couldn't have made it through the winter.

It is evening—any evening of the week—and it seems that all the living rooms, dining rooms, strongboxes, and china cabinets in Hamburg have been turned out in this park. Cameras, table linens, heirlooms. Women in head scarves and calf-high leather boots displaying silverware. Young men in Wermacht field caps with guns for sale under greatcoats. Old men, stony-faced, ramrod straight, in neckties, frayed white shirts, and worn suitcoats, holding up the family candlesticks.

Air force blue and British Army khaki swirl slowly through this motley crowd, looking for something to buy or just *looking*—at something poignant and pitiful: a bazaar of lost pride.

This park does not buzz with commerce. No small talk, no gaiety. Often, just eye contact and a mute offering of goods. A few vendors in slick leather coats and pasted-on smiles are polished black marketeers, hustling us with fake bonhommie. But many more of the faces are sullen, shut-in, bitter. More still are grim, eyes sorrowful. For them, I think, this is a night of desperation and humiliation. Their hopes and dreams and once-upon-a-times are spread naked under the gloomy sky.

And yet . . . these people, given different clothes and a smile or two, could have been my neighbors on Shamrock's main street. I was torn with confusion. *How must it feel to have to flog the family silver? What if my mother had to peddle her primrose dinnerware?* But these were the same people who condoned the awful sights in those Belsen photographs. Some of these young men in German greatcoats were probably *there.*

So began a winter of wild paradox, as I drifted to and fro between the base and the painful realities beyond it. The days were usually dank and chilly, the sky slate gray, lending the whole region an air of gloom and foreboding. No wonder the Jerries tried to conquer the world, joked the 443 Squadron "diary" (a brief listing of daily events); they wanted to escape their climate.

Remnants of German clung to our hangar walls—"RAUCHEN VERBOTEN" (Smoking Forbidden). The runways and taxi strips were sheets of perforated metal matting, like Swiss cheese, an instant portable airfield designed for rough situations. At Uetersen it covered acres of mud that oozed up through the metal pores. I knew Saskatchewan gumbo (from those rare prairie years when we were lucky enough to *have* mud) but this was world-class mud.

Our pilots flew whenever the weather was fit. In October, they spent several days at cine gun exercises (simulated shooting), flew a sortie over Hamburg "to impress the Germans," escorted a transfer of German aircraft from another base, and took part in a Wing flyover at Schleswig, sixty miles north.

Each morning we clomped down to the hangar in khaki coveralls and rubber boots, to the thrumming of motors and familiar fumes of oil and gas. I checked my Spit's rudder, ailerons, and anything else that moved, gave tires and hydraulic legs the once-over, got the pilot into his seat, plugged in a booster motor to help start the engine, pulled the chocks away from the wheels, and waved him out to the runway. When he came home I guided him into his parking spot, set the chocks, refueled from the bowser, and called it a day. I was a less nervous mechanic now, through experience, my affection for Spitfires, and the fact that not much ever went wrong with them.

They march through the pages of a tattered photo album, those ground crew men of 443. Names and faces dimly remembered . . . Herb Mills, Kernie Kernahan, Roly Marriott, Andy Asseltine, Duffield, Franks, Fraser, Gamble, Little, Russell . . .

Where are you now? Do you ever think back to that time and place? The card games and endless yarning and binding in the back room? "Tea up" from the Canadian Legion War Services truck? Schnapps-the-wiener-dog, our dachshund mascot? Bud Townsend crying "Let's get a whole keg of beer and drink it *all* up!", his face shining with pleasure at the thought? And the day Joe Fink, engine mechanic, was warming up a Spit at high revs, head down in the cockpit, enjoying the motor's song, when the tail went up, the nose tipped down, the prop bit through snow just an inch away from the metal taxi strip, and Joe was just an inch away from being an AC2 again?

And how, through all the laughs and waiting, we wondered if and when we'd ever get on with the rest of our lives?

Chapter Twelve

The RCAF caste system, like a sliver under the thumbnail, was always there. In the beginning I had accepted it, passively and pragmatically. Now it was more and more of an irritant to me and to most of my fellows. The relaxed environment of BAFO was giving us a taste for civilian life. And, in more than two years of service, we'd discovered that—man for man—officers were no better than we. Yet without better education or being in air crew, we would never attain their rank, with its better clothes, better food, better pay, and its salutes from the lower classes. We were the poor in the low-rent district; they were the upper class.

Keen ground crew types—and there *were* a few—were on pseudo-chummy terms with their pilots on the flight line (it didn't extend beyond that). I and most others were not. Once a new pilot was assigned to "my" 21X. He was dark and sharp-eyed with a lean intelligent face; not much older than I but with the officer's air of confidence, authority, and elitism that I envied and resented. I guessed I was as intelligent as he, but felt inferior by the very nature of my job and rank.

He made some friendly small talk about 21X and me. He'd heard, correctly, that having the mechanic on his side was an asset. I was suspicious, polite, and otherwise unresponsive. Maybe camaraderie between the ranks had existed during the shooting war but more likely, I thought cynically, it was the phony good will of the estate manager toward his field hands.

So, rightly or wrongly, I kept on doing my job at arm's length. The pilot needn't have worried; I was as eager to keep him alive as he was. We dared never forget that their lives depended on us.

On the morning of November 9 the squadrons went up as usual. Around the hangars we settled in for a tea break and games of hearts or darts in the ground crew rooms. Suddenly an alarm raced through the base: a kite had pranged. Instantly every mechanic's heart leaped to his throat. *Was it our squadron? One of our guys? How bad? Was it my fault?*

Dozens of us piled into trucks to search the scrub bush in the surrounding countryside. By the time my party reached the scene they'd found him, a flying officer from 416. His motor had cut out soon after takeoff. We stood mutely beside the crumpled Spit while they loaded the dead boy into an ambulance. I stared at his boots, sticking out from under the blanket on the stretcher. *What a stupid waste, that he should die in this nonwar.* A stillness hung over the base the rest of that day and night. His death rated one line in the daily diary.

We lived in former Luftwaffe barracks, three or four men to frigid rooms in three-storey brick buildings. Rarely was there heat or hot water; rumor said somebody had sold our coal ration on the black market. Showers were swift and cursory, we wore leather jerkins over our tunics and we burrowed into bed in long underwear. Joe Fink slept with three blankets under him and one over (we never had sheets), to cut off the Arctic drafts from the floor. At least there was no inspection, of rooms or men. It was *almost* like a civilian job, which ultimately made us yearn for civvy street all the more.

There were movies nearly every night and frequent traveling stage shows starring pretty girls who sang and danced for us all, then went to parties in the officers' mess. I poured out letters to Canada and another to Ireland. Finally Connie Macnab sent a note in scrunched childlike handwriting, friendly but not loving as I'd hoped and expected. I read and re-read it, hurt and puzzled, looking for omens. Perhaps she was just shy and inarticulate on paper? Or . . . had her feelings changed? I didn't want to find that out by mail. In the spring, I'd get leave, go back to Ireland, and settle it. For now I tried to push her from my mind, which was difficult, with her picture always in my sterling silver wrist locket.

One Saturday we trucked down the Autobahn to Bremen to watch a U.S. servicemen's football game. Football bored me but there were free hot dogs. A large friendly GI offered me a stick of Spearmint.

"Bet it's a long time since you had that!" he said, in the manner of Champlain offering beads to the Hurons. He so obviously wanted to be liked—*look what bountiful America can provide!*—that

I didn't have the heart to tell him the Shamrock Women's Auxiliary and the Bateman Canadian Legion shipped me more Spearmint, Doublemint, and Juicy Fruit than my jaws could handle.

"Tastes good," I said, truthfully. He beamed with satisfaction. Was Connie Macnab's American also free with largesse? After all, he was a captain, and had his own Jeep . . . Was she still seeing him? Americans! *Officers!*

In November, their daily diary noted, 443 Squadron pilots "were soundly defeated by a team of erks in a rather rough [soccer] game." For the airmen it was a glorious opportunity to work the officers over without fear of a week in the digger. The depressing aura of Hamburg was beginning to get to us. So was the officers' habit of calling us "erks" with, it seemed to us, thinly veiled contempt.

One night several of them climbed into a three-ton truck to go to Hamburg. A number of "erks" (as they complained later) piled on too, outnumbering the officers two to one. The 443 daily diary of November 17 told the pitiful tale.

> A long crowded uncomfortable ride into town and back hardly makes the pleasure derived from dinner and a few drinks at the Atlantic Officers Club worthwhile. To see German civilian workers travelling in a bus and German Army officers driving their own cars only adds insult to injury.

Three nights later, the officers got their own bus so they would not have to ride with the unwashed masses. We "erks" had been riding in the backs of three-ton trucks since the war began. We waited stoically for the day when officers got back to the real world.

The author of that diary entry saw, with his particular myopia, *some* Germans driving cars. But hundreds more were riding bikes or were packed like anchovies onto streetcars and trains until they hung out the windows and clung to the footrails. Some were *flüchtlinge* (refugees) from the East, living six to a single room or in a basement with no light or heat. The people of Hamburg were fighting for their lives.

The Occupation authorities faced a problem. Should they help the Germans get back on their feet, or let them suffer for Nazi sins? (Few Germans would admit that those were *their* sins.)

In the end, there was no choice. It would have been grossly unfair, and political suicide in Europe, to be nice to the Jerries that winter. At the Potsdam Conference of victors in July, it was ruled that Germans must not live better than the rest of Europe. A minimum ration of 1,550 calories per German per day was prescribed but in practice it was less. More than 4.2 million tons of coal were dug from the Ruhr Valley in October, but it was earmarked for troops like us and for the people of the Netherlands, Norway, and Denmark. Not one lump went to German civilians.

So they lived by their wits, scrounging wood from the rubble, dealing on the black market. I met them often there but superficially. The war was still too close for friendship. Most of us picked up bits of the language far more readily than in Quebec. Here there was incentive. Although many Hamburg people spoke a little English, a word or two of German helped an airman function on the market.

- What're you selling?
- *Bitte?* [Please?]
- What you got to sell? *Verstehen sie?* [Do you understand?] *Sprechen sie englisch?*
- *Ja.* You want kamera?
- Maybe. *Wieviel?* [How much?]
- Iss *gut!* Leica!
- Yeah, sure. *Wieviel?*
- *Haben sie zigaretten?*
- Sure, I've got cigarettes. *Wieviel?*
- *Funftausend. Verstehen sie?* Fife T-ousand.
- Five thousand! *Nein, nein. Nicht gut!*

We bicker and bargain and settle on three thousand cigarettes.

Our small green military-government paper marks or the big tattered deutsche marks were of no interest on the market. Cigarettes were the currency of the day. We bought them cheap or got free cartons from generous people and organizations back home. With cigarettes I bought a camera, a pair of naval binoculars, a Mauser handgun that wouldn't shoot, a German officer's ceremonial sword, an indestructible plywood suitcase, and handfuls of military insignia, including three Iron Crosses and a charming blue pin that Hitler awarded to good Aryan girls for having babies.

The Germans were not crazed for nicotine; they bartered our cigarettes for food, fuel, and other necessities. Tailor-mades were better than money. Some American GIs, we heard, got their kicks by tossing whole cigarettes onto the sidewalk, then jerking them back on a string when passing Jerries dove for them—as they always did.

It was relatively easy, in our nest of comforts, to ignore what was happening around us. In the Canada Club, run by the Canadian Legion, an airman could dine, write letters, get a haircut, listen to music, and catch a ride back to Uetersen without ever talking to a German. A few did just that. Complete meals sold for three marks (thirty cents). In one typical month, we devoured 13,537 hamburgers, 25,000 pastries, 3,786 orders of pork and beans on toast, and gallons of tea, coffee, Coke, and the favorite canned fruit juice. Outside, the Jerries were scrabbling for their 1,550 calories.

I didn't grasp the full extent of the drama around us; years later, I would curse myself for not keeping a journal. But I was aware of my emotional dilemma, and never really resolved it. I had arrived with no sympathy for the Germans. I felt that our Hamburg Nazis (or former Nazis, or never-were Nazis) were getting their just desserts. Our side (apart from the ruthless Russians) was treating them better than Hitler's conquerors had treated occupied Europe. But as we ignored the nonfraternization order and prowled the city with lively curiosity, I kept seeing not the German nation but *individuals*, beaten yet sometimes proud and still defiant.

Most of the males were in mix-and-match clothes, maybe civilian trousers and a uniform tunic or greatcoat stripped of insignia. The young ones hated us; it burned in their eyes. We were air force; the air force had decimated Hamburg. The pragmatic older men and women disguised their hatred, thanked God we weren't Russians, and turned our humane instincts to their advantage. They were servile, respectful, friendly as occasion dictated. The young women could handle us with a smile, and knew it.

"Schlafen sie mit mir, fraulein?" murmurs the airman, proud of his first German phrase.

"Haben sie zigaretten?" she counters, coyly. It is the beginning of a beautiful, if short-lived, friendship.

One night a fellow airman and I picked up two frauleins outside the Canada Club. Among the immutable laws of service life were

1. Girls travel in pairs, a pretty one and an ugly one.
2. Your friend will always get the pretty one.

110

On this frosty evening my companion, a short fellow with a ruddy cherubic face, swiftly led the pretty one to the girls' single room in a broken-down building.

"Come back in about half an hour," he murmured, nudge-nudge-wink-wink. "Then I'll take this one out for a walk and *you* can have the room."

My girl—flaxen haired, pleasant, and overweight—walked with me through the snowy streets, making shivering small talk. She was fluent in English. She had no interest in casual sex and I was in love with Connie Macnab. We were both nearly frozen when the half-hour was up. Back at the room, my beaming friend pressed cigarettes and chocolate bars into the pretty one's hand, I said good night to the big one, and we caught the truck back to camp.

A number of airmen had permanent girlfriends off base and occasionally smuggled one into the barracks for an overnighter. (There were ways to get past the guardhouse.) A small randy mechanic from our hangar regularly spent nights with his mistress in town. Her husband had gone missing on the Russian front, meaning he was dead or, worse, in a Russian prison camp. Our man consoled the wife with regular gifts of coal and food, in return for conjugal rights.

Sometimes he came to work in the husband's handsome leather jacket. We reminded him that if the Jerry unexpectedly came home some night, hardened and mean from prison camp labor, it would be game over for one nude Canadian. He just chuckled and went back for more. Whatever his morals, he was closer to the German people than I.

My closest friend was Herb Gallifent, a freckled, ginger-haired instrument mechanic from Hamilton, Ontario. He was thoroughly sweet tempered—his strongest epithet was "blinkin' "—and no more predatory than I. One night as we roamed the park, cartons of barter stuffed in our shoulder bags, he negotiated a camera for three thousand cigarettes from two young women. They didn't want to carry so much black market exchange for fear of being nabbed by the police. Would we walk them home and hand over the cigarettes? We did.

Home was a single room in a dilapidated house, sparsely furnished but with pathetic little touches of femininity. Rather than leave it as a cold-blooded transaction, they invited us to sit down. Perhaps they were hoping for a long-term relationship or maybe they were just curious about Canadians and looking for friendly company on a bleak winter night.

We *were* friendly, no more nor less. In time, we might have parlayed it into more. But we sensed they were nice girls — their tentative manner and the plainness of their clothes and their flat attested to that — and we treated them with old-fashioned courtesy. It was a sweet-sad scene, rather like a high school date. We talked and laughed in broken German and English. They played records on their old hand-cranked phonograph. Then we politely shook hands and said good night.

We never saw them again. Often, in after years, I remembered that evening with a twist of the heart for four lonely young people on opposite sides of the war who reached out but never quite touched.

Chapter Thirteen

Peek into the 416 Squadron Orderly Room any day between dawn and dusk and you will usually find [Cpl. Jimmy Groom] bending over his typewriter. . . . His first move after arrival home will be a short march up the aisle with a young lady who is waiting anxiously for his return. After that, we assume that the bride and Groom will live happily ever after.

This forgettable prose with its awful pun was mine, and I relished every syllable. I'd discovered *Canocc,* the RCAF weekly newspaper at Uetersen. Some of my pieces appeared as "Hangnail Sketches," this one on January 12, 1946.

At last I was working in journalism, of sorts. Being editor of the Shamrock High School sheet (written in longhand and cranked out on a duplicator with purple ink) and being Shamrock stringer for the Regina *Leader-Post* at ten cents an inch didn't really count. In November 1945 the newly established *Canocc* appealed for editorial help and I shyly applied. They tried me out on a story and by the next issue I was on the masthead as "staff writer."

It was a volunteer job, with no time off from the hangar, but it did wonders for my state of mind. *Canocc* was a lively little tabloid and, at one-half mark (five cents) a copy, everyone read it. I wrote personality sketches and small features. My writing style was no worse than the rest. My friends, if not impressed, were at least intrigued. And *Canocc* was the first democracy I'd found anywhere in the RCAF: the editor, Bill Williams, was a corporal, the art editor and production manager were LACs, the sports editor was a flight lieutenant, the staff photographer was a sergeant, and my fellow staff writer was a squadron leader named Harback. There were no "sirs" or salutes.

I particularly warmed to LAC Bill McVean, a control tower operator when he wasn't features editor of *Canocc* and broadcaster on CAF, our own radio station operated from a barracks block attic. McVean, a witty fellow a few months younger than I, was likewise weary of his air force lot. He'd enlisted with a private pilot's license, found his eyesight didn't meet RCAF standards, and ended up on the ground. Even so, having joined 126 Wing shortly after D-day, he'd seen far more of the war than I.

A few months earlier, he'd even been co-owner of a German Junkers bomber — briefly. One night, deep in Germany near war's end, McVean and another airman were on duty on the Wing's airstrip when a plane landed. They thought it was one of their own, until the swastika on its tail and crosses on its sides loomed out of the dusk. Five Germans jumped out with their hands up. McVean and his partner were unarmed, but faked it until the service police took over.

By war's unofficial rule of thumb, if you "liberated" something, it was yours. McVean felt the omens were excellent when their commanding officer asked, "Can I look at it?" and, a little later, "What're you going to do with it?"

"Maybe we could use it to fly the boys back to the coast on leave?" suggested McVean. Good idea, the CO thought, and a generous gesture on McVean's part. Then a senior RAF officer liberated the Junkers as his own personal plane and McVean went back to his control tower.

But not entirely. At *Canocc* he wrote a column (funnier than most of our alleged humor) and turned me loose on "Hangnail Sketches," a collection of short profiles. Soon I was generating my own ideas. I bought a thundering old manual typewriter on the black market — it printed only capital letters and gave me German umlauts when I wanted semicolons — and pounded out short features in my frigid room, wrapped in my leather jerkin. One story was about the kids from Heist.

December 30. We are lounging in somebody's barracks room, sharing a premature New Year's Eve drink and waiting for the evening movie. A timid knock at the door.
"Come in!"
With a burst of German song and the squawk of an accordion, a half-dozen costumed youngsters file in. One of them totes a sack. Two others, forming the front and rear of a white cloth horse, perform a little dance. What nerve

114

it took, and how many whispered consultations, to brave this "enemy" camp! These aren't Nazis; they're grinning little kids, like those back home.

We applaud them heartily and joke with them in two broken languages. They are six to twelve years old, from the nearby village of Heist. This is an annual year-end custom, rather like our Halloween. We fill their bag with chewing gum, chocolate bars, Lifesavers, and spare pfennigs.

"Auf Wiedersehen!" we call. They giggle, wave goodbye, and, led by the horse, gallop off to the next room. Afterward, I feel better than at any time since we came to Germany.

All through that holiday season we didn't lack for entertainment. On Christmas Eve girls from the military government in Hamburg came on base singing carols, and a Santa Claus gave cigarettes and a parcel to each man. On Christmas Day the officers and sergeants served us the traditional turkey dinner. On Boxing Day, a German concert party sang for us. Three days later we enjoyed the spectacle of new pilots being checked out on Spits.

"All the airmen gathered in front of the hangar to watch the fun," reported the daily diary. "Sgt. McIntosh and Cpl. Bates had a gun ready for everybody that pranged a kite." Nobody did. We were proud of our squadron; it racked up 377 flying hours that month, more than any other, and later was rated the best in BAFO.

I spent New Year's Eve on the base. Neither Hamburg's misery nor the creature comforts of the Canada Club were appealing that night. A good dance band was playing in the cinema but there were no spare girls to dance with. We partied with beer and schnapps from mess hall to canteen to various noisy rooms, with sodden toasts of "Here's to home in '46 — maybe?" At midnight the sky lit up, not with fireworks but with tracer bullets from our rifles. I came closer to getting shot that peacetime night than any other time during the war.

The safest place was inside the brick barracks. I went there with Herb Gallifent and Joe Fink. Joe, the farm boy from unforgettable Plunkett, Saskatchewan, was a droll fellow with a generous nose and a deadpan expression that hid volumes of latent mischief. My final memory of New Year's Eve was Fink on his bunk in his longjohns, firing streams of tracers out the window to greet 1946, while Gallifent and I cheered him on. Later, Joe didn't remember it.

Schnapps, a sharp-tasting liquor from the gin family, had a powerful kick which we sometimes modified with beer chasers

(Fink claimed the watery German beer sobered you up). It was important to drink the genuine stuff, not the cheap and lethal moonshine which had poisoned many Uetersen airmen and killed several Yanks in the American Zone. Gallifent found a way to guarantee real schnapps: he insisted that the vendor take a swallow first.

There was more drinking on this station than any I'd known. It was an antidote to ennui and to the pervasive gloom of Hamburg and its plight. Most men were too hungover to get up Sunday morning. Those of us with moderate drinking habits and excessive appetites hastened to the mess hall and heaped our plates with fresh fried eggs the cooks somehow scrounged for Sunday breakfast. Other days, food on the base was like mess hall food anywhere.

"Can't help you, pal," said one of the mess crew, when asked to name a shapeless item in the steam trays. "We only cook the stuff, not identify it."

The canteen with its chocolate bars, the Canada Club with sandwiches and hamburgers, and our occasional parcels from home filled the empty spaces in our yawning stomachs. Joe Fink's mother, like mine, often sent homemade cookies. His always disintegrated on the journey, perhaps because heavy jars of home-canned chicken traveled in the same box. It didn't matter. We ate every crumb.

We did not talk about the wild extremes between our diets and the Jerries'; that the leftovers in our mess hall would have been a feast for those kids from the village of Heist. Even if I had thought of sharing my bounty with some of them—and in truth I can not say I did—it would have been an unpopular sentiment among most of my peers, and a breach of discipline. (The men who smuggled food and fuel to their mistresses would have been in trouble, if caught.)

The Germans had lost the war. The peace was a mere eight months old; memories were still fresh and bitter. If their rations were thin, "tough shit." This was their punishment. They were better off than the inmates of Buchenwald and Belsen had ever been.

I discovered "educational leave": a week of mind improvement at air force expense. In January I was off like a shot for Paris to join forty other air force and army men and women of many ranks at *La Maison Canadienne,* a big white house commandeered for lodgings and study courses. I linked up with three new LACs:

a taciturn fellow named Lewis, Red Duff with his fine sleek cap of cinnamon-colored hair, and Al Stemmler with a young man's face and a bald head.

We heard lectures on French history and culture, and saw every landmark—the Eiffel Tower, Notre Dame, the Arc de Triomphe, Montmartre, Mona Lisa in the Louvre, bare bosoms in the Folies Bergere, and hookers on Rue Pigalle.

One night we were offered an evening with a French family. I was parceled off with two army boys from Quebec. Our hosts were gracious, dinner was good, but I spent the evening desperately keeping my chin above the conversational waters. The Quebecers plunged eagerly into French, which pleased our hosts since the husband spoke no English. I dared not try out the words that my grade ten teacher, Miss Dempson, and I had mispronounced together.

Occasionally Madame turned to me with a pitying smile. "You don' speak *any* French?" My facial muscles ached from smiling, to prove I was having fun and *almost* understanding. Oddly, by evening's end—my first experience in French immersion—I almost *did*.

The next day, mentally drained but proud of my effort, I strolled beside the Seine, watched an artist at work with his easel, and pinched myself. Me, *really* in Paris! *How you gonna keep 'em down in Shamrock, after they've seen Paree? . . .*

A photographer bullied us into group portraits, so he could sell us enlarged prints. In most of them I was bareheaded. I had acquired an irrational dislike of my wedge cap; going without it was a petty defiance of the military. I carried it in my dress tunic belt or battle dress shoulder strap and, when caught, was ticked off. On the way back to Germany with a two-day stop in Brussels, my errant hat found a life of its own.

My friends of the moment and I are at a dance. Some primitive jungle telegraph always enables us to find the most popular bar, the nearest dance, the favored source of girls in strange cities. So, here I am in Brussels, a farm boy lately of Shamrock, jogging mechanically around the floor with a small sweet-eyed Belgian girl.

"You speak English?" I ask. After years of standing mute in the presence of girls, I am now famed for my dazzling repartee.

"Jus' a li'l bit," she says. *My God! She has learned to speak*

117

English with a Dixie accent. Am I cursed to follow in the tracks of Yanks, wherever I go?

Still, we're having fun and dancing very close. My libido is high but, having patronized several bars, my reflexes are sluggish. Suddenly Miss Brussels of 1945 is gone, and so is my wedge cap. Why would she? . . . Finally, through a faint cognac haze, I conclude that she collects military hat badges for fun and profit. I get back to Hamburg by hiding out whenever service police are around.

Forty years later I watch a Monty Python skit about a salacious wench who lures milkmen to her room and *keeps* them forever. Suddenly I visualize a Belgian woman chuckling into her sunset years surrounded by a roomful of badges. "And here," she tells her grandchildren, "is the one a nice Canadian airman gave to me because he loved me so very much. . . ."

Uetersen was in two inches of snow. We sprayed glycol on the hinges of Spitfire rudders, flaps, and ailerons to keep them from freezing, and the pilots kept flying. The squadron now had thirty-five Spits and in January completed 381 flying hours, the most since the Occupation began. Not all were uneventful. One day F/L Nick Rassenti, with two others from 443, was flying north of the Kaiser Wilhelm Canal when a Thunderbolt—literally—hit him. The U.S. Army Air Force plane from a base at nearby Nordholz dived out of the sky and sheared off Rassenti's wing.

His Spit burst into flames and rolled on its back. Rassenti managed to bail out and was back at Uetersen by afternoon, with only a few cuts and bruises. The American pilot also survived. There were high-level discussions between the Yanks and our own top brass, but I never learned the outcome.

A day later there was a real tragedy: the pilots' bus broke down on the way to Hamburg, but our officers managed to soldier through. "Rather than ride back to camp in the back of a three-ton truck, the boys spent the night at the Atlantic Club in Hamburg," the January 19 daily diary soberly reported.

By now we'd had a visit and a speech from Colonel Colin Gibson, Canada's minister of national defence. The question on everyone's mind—when do we go home?—went unanswered. Gibson didn't know. It was partly a problem of acquiring enough trans-Atlantic shipping, and getting the long-service men home first. In England, early in February, eight hundred RCAF ground crew in Gloucestershire and twelve hundred in Hampshire took matters into their own hands: they went on strike, protesting poor rations and slowness in repatriation. RAF personnel in India and the Middle and Far East had already set the precedent. The Canadian strikes ended in a few days, after threats and promises from high command.

The idea of *striking* was beyond my comprehension. My father would have disowned me if I had. In our home, strikes and strikers were dirty words. Anyway, I'd signed up to serve, and a deal was a deal. But what good *was* the Occupation? Few of us realized the value of keeping a presence in Germany to face Russia; to most North Americans, Russia was still the friendly ally. As for quelling the Germans: they had no stomach for war that winter.

So we languished in boredom. I wrote one more letter to Connie Macnab, received no answer, and withdrew in a sulk. In December and in February we took mandatory trade tests. I didn't study, and scored seventy the first time and sixty-five the second, neither mark good enough to promote me into "A" group and an extra twenty-five cents a day. Writing for *Canocc* was far more important to me than being a better mechanic. Others—except Sam Glassford, who was now a corporal—were similarly unmotivated. The NCO who conducted the test was exasperated.

"I don't understand you men," he snapped at me. "Don't you care? You're not going home for a long time."

We *didn't* care. We were gradually infected by the despair and decadence around us. (A few men, turning the black market into a lucrative industry, didn't *want* to go home.) Around the flight line we became a raffish-looking lot: muddy boots, greasy coveralls, toques, jerkins, and false-front woollen turtleneck tops, disguising the absence of shirts underneath. Half proudly, half cynically, we referred to the scruffiest among us as "operational types."

Conversely, off duty we were dandies. German barbers cultivated our longer hairstyles, defty trimmed our eyebrows with straight razors, and talcumed our faces. After one such treatment a Jerry photographer took my portrait, and retouched lines and blemishes. I looked like a dummy in Madame Tussaud's Wax Museum. German tailors created for some of us a hybrid battle dress—blouse tunic with flat lapels, similar to American uniforms. It was strictly against regulations but we got through the guardhouse wearing greatcoats and unveiled our new finery once safely past the gates.

119

Certain areas of Hamburg, noted for prostitutes and thugs, were designated "out of bounds." Naturally we had to go there. One night four of us, fired up with schnapps, explored the sector. (Two years before, such flaunting of rules would have been unthinkable for me.) Having seen too many Humphrey Bogart movies, we went with delicious expectation of danger. One man had a black market Luger in his tunic. I, feeling foolish, had a version of a Swiss army knife up my sleeve. A pompous medical orderly joined our entourage clutching a loaded revolver in his pocket.

We swaggered into a dance with our tailored lapels, the only foreigners in a sea of giggling young women and cold-eyed men in discarded German uniforms.

"Keep your eyes open, men!" muttered the silly orderly, making menacing motions inside his pocket.

Floating on a pungent wave of schnapps, we swept female partners onto the floor. The young men gazed at us with open malice, but were not inclined to start a ruckus: our SPs and the civilian cops, if called to the scene, would have caused the Jerries even more grief than us. The girls found us amusing, and wonderfully generous with cigarettes. I was sporting my Blankenberge dagger lapel pin.

"*Was ist das?*" inquired my dance partner.

"Kommando!" said the schnapps, which was doing the talking for me. She tinkled with laughter, in admiration or because she saw through my whopper. Luckily, as we sobered up, prudence took over and we got out before any former Gestapo in our audience yielded to temptation, or before our puffed-up orderly could shoot himself in the foot.

Soon the same orderly came up with the most ingenious sex scam of the winter. A group of local girls was swept up for a VD check by our medical department. The orderly came to me aglow with triumph.

"Listen, I'm taking the names and addresses of all the clean ones, and best looking ones," he cried. "Then you and me'll take 'em some cigarettes and chocolate, and we'll be set for the winter!"

It was clever, but too coldblooded.

"Nah. Not interested."

"You crazy? This is a *sure thing!*"

"Yeah, probably is."

He pouted. "Listen, if you don't go along with this I'm not gonna be your friend any more!"

"Tough!" I said. We never spoke again.

We rolled through February into March, the air full of snow and rumors. There was still no word on total repatriation but individuals with long service were already going home. On the way to breakfast one morning I met a friend, just in from town and falling-down drunk.

"I got laid last night and I'm going home tomorrow!" he shouted. I wished him well on both counts, privately hoping he wasn't taking VD home to his wife.

A hundred Danish girls from No. 3 District Censorship Station came to frolic with the officers at our base. About the same time, the British Zone announced the German ration would be cut to 1,014 calories a day. By April, a spokesman said, "People will be without bread or potatoes and will be dying in the streets in very large numbers."

There were other small deaths. One afternoon as I stood alone outside the Canada Club with my brain in neutral, a stunning dark-eyed young woman approached me, clearly distraught.

"Do you know_____?" she said in stiffly proper English, and named an LAC.

By chance I knew him well.

"He was to meet me last night and did not."

"I'm sorry," I said, as kindly as I knew how, "but he was posted home, day before yesterday."

She stared at me for a long moment, then went away without another word, crying softly. I watched her small figure disappear among the shattered streets, thinking: *It is time we all went home.*

On the afternoon of March 11, the station group captain called us all into the cinema to say 126 Wing was closing up shop. The Spits would be flown to England; ground crew would return by land and water. Bill Williams had already gone home; McVean was editor of *Canocc,* with me due to become features editor. But going back to Britain (and Connie, I hoped) and, eventually, home was better.

The end came quickly. On March 22, after a full night of schnapps, we turned in our rifles and packed our kit bags and black market loot. Joe Fink asked us to scribble our names for posterity on the flyleaf of his engine mechanics' handbook. His friend Gamble, memory fresh from the previous night, signed it from the one "who helped you back to camp." I took the carriage off my big German typewriter, wrapped it and the base of the machine in two padded parcels, crossed my fingers, and mailed them home to Shamrock. The post office, true to form, demolished both.

Two nights before we left, twenty German women broke into some Hamburg food shops and fled with loaves of bread and sacks of flour. In the Tiefstack railway yards two hundred others broke into boxcars and stole bags of oats. The British called up armored cars and chased the "rioters" off with a few shots in the air. The day we left, thirty-three workmen in the railway machine shops collapsed from hunger.

> Each [military occupation throughout history] has resulted slowly but inexorably in the defeat of the victorious power . . . . Occupation of a country though it may castigate the vanquished, degrades the victor . . . . The defeat of an occupation begins when the war that brought it ends . . . .
>
> Anonymous RAF airman writing in *Harper's Magazine*, November 1945

Chapter Fourteen

We lurched across the North Sea from Cuxhaven, on the German north coast, aboard the *Empire Rapier*. The North Sea is not kind to small boats and it was no trip for people who'd been guzzling schnapps for much of the previous forty-eight hours. We landed at Hull, tired, grubby, seasick, and surly.

The trains and trucks dumped us out at RCAF station Topcliffe back on the Yorkshire moors. A day later we moved fifteen miles down the road to RCAF Leeming. The honeymoon for "operational types" was over. Our feet were hardly off the trucks before an RAF officer with a mouth like two halves of a muffin chided us about dirty shirt collars. We stared back stonily, barely containing our hostility. *Fuggin' pongo! We just got off a North Sea bucket, how about lending us your batman to do our laundry?* Then, who should appear on morning parade but our old friend Flight Sergeant Shaw, lately of TTS, St. Thomas. He was not so friendly this day.

"YOU MEN," he said, in a conversational shout that scattered a flock of sheep in a dale five miles east, "are the SLOPPIEST, SCRUFFIEST types I've ever seen! You are a DISGRACE to the service. Oh, I know you're just back from the Continent, but you're still in the AIR FORCE. I don't want to see ANY more nonregulation uniforms. I don't want to see HAIR growing down your COLLARS. And I want to see CLEAN battle dress TOMORROW MORNING! Get at it with gasoline! GET CRACKING!"

We did. It was actually a relief to have somebody lay down the law again, a sort of post-Hamburg antidote. But even Shaw couldn't talk us out of the air force blues. We went on filling time with joe-jobs, afternoons off, overnight passes, and long weekends. I tracked down old friends on neighboring stations: Smitty,

Kuh-nurled Kuh-nob, and Al Cooper, who'd been in England eighteen months and was panting for his girl in Winnipeg. I took another trade test, scored only seventy, and for the third time failed to get "A" group.

It didn't matter. My only priorities were seeing Connie Macnab and going home, in that order. With a seven-day leave in the offing, I wrote her to say I was on my way. Still no reply. I left for Ireland, alone, one April night with a sense of foreboding. In seven months I'd had that single noncommittal letter. It was ominous.

As soon as I got off the overnight boat, I phoned her office. She was expecting me; we could meet after work. She looked even more irresistible, a trifle fuller of form; over the winter she seemed to have blossomed from girl to young woman. It took only a minute to notice the diamond on her left hand, and five minutes more to swallow the pain and conjure up enough feigned calm to murmur, "So you're wearing a ring!" Hoping it was a mistake.

"Why yes, didn't I write you about it?" she said awkwardly, knowing she hadn't. "It's the American fellow I told you about last summer."

I was crushed. She, not an insensitive girl, was almost as miserable as I. Her American had gone home, she explained, but would send for her in the autumn. The evening was ruined. A little later I said stiffly, "Guess I'll cut my leave short and go home tomorrow. Not much point in staying."

"You don't have to," she said worriedly. Then added kindly, "It would be nice if you could stay." But she didn't *beg* me to stay, as I had hoped. Kindness, I didn't need.

But I stayed, because I was madly in love, because I was ashamed to face my friends in defeat, and because secretly I hoped somehow to change her mind. We went riding, skating, dancing, and to church with her family to hear the "Messiah." And because we genuinely enjoyed each other, it was *almost* as much fun as before. But the good night kisses were brief and chaste. If I had not been hurting so much, I would have admired her for that, too.

The word seemed to have raced through her female friends' grapevine that Connie had ditched her Canadian and it was open season. One of them planned a goodbye party for me, but inadvertently set it a day late—the day I was due back in camp. Two years before, I'd have dutifully returned. This time I wired

Leeming: "FIANCEE ILL. REQUEST EXTRA DAY LEAVE." Any smart orderly room clerk knew that if Fiancee was *really* ill I'd have asked for more than one day. But back came a tolerant "EXTENSION GRANTED" and I went to the party with Connie.

As the only male in uniform, and a Canadian, I was the object of some attention. *I'll make her jealous! Then she'll realize what she's losing!* I chatted up every girl in sight, using a palm-reading act I'd recently invented for such occasions. As a boy I had once sent away boxtops for a booklet on palmistry. I knew the head line from the heart line and the life line from the Mount of Venus. From there on I winged it, making up outrageous predictions and character analyses, while nestling each tender palm in my own.

Whether or not they knew it was hokum, they loved it. Their Belfast boyfriends were furious. Had the group not all been former school friends, the young men might have taken me into an alley and given me the backs of *their* palms.

After many drinks and more harmless games, somebody turned out the lights and couples paired off, with much laughter and rustling. I found myself kissing and fondling a young woman with long dark hair, heroic breasts, and no special boyfriend. She had particularly enjoyed her palm reading, especially when I predicted for her a vibrant social life. I was persuading myself that I could forget Connie Macnab when her voice came plaintively from the dark.

"Bob? Where are you?"

Devotedly, I went to her. As the other girl gave me up, she whispered bitterly, "Connie always gets what she wants!"

After the party I said goodbye to Connie, swiftly, almost impersonally. Two of the boyfriends dropped me off at the Legion hostel, glad to see the last of me. In the morning I left Belfast, never to return.

I made up my mind to forget. My constant companions— Cooper, Gallifent, and Jim Williams, a flaxen-haired six-footer from British Columbia—had struck gold: a dance "club" in Bradford, a small city about sixty miles south-west. For two shillings admission, anyone could "join" for an evening. Miraculously, the Yanks hadn't discovered it, perhaps because it was an unpretentious second-floor room with no twirling sparkling centerpiece in the ceiling, as in most great dance palaces in the major cities.

Even more incredible, women patrons outnumbered the men—and during the dances *they* cut in! I turned into a dancing fool. I twirled around the floor with an endless procession of girls who loved to dance, or talk, or flirt, or all three. I danced with silent girls who plastered their every curve of hip and thigh, every swell of breast, against my agitated self, then wordlessly melted away when the music stopped. Sometimes I was passed, willingly, among three different partners during one number. And there one night I danced with Vera Taylor.

She was seventeen, small and slender, with a white smile and enormous dark dancing eyes, almost a dead ringer for Hollywood's sweetheart-of-the-moment, Judy Garland.

"Ah'm thin as a rake!" she'd say disparagingly of herself in her Yorkshire accent. She was *not* as hefty as most of her friends—a distinct asset. Every inch of her, as I came to know, was exquisitely formed and fine.

Our flirtation turned serious. We spent every weekend together—at movies, dances, walks in the park, fish and chip suppers from a twist of newspaper, pints of half-and-half and shandy in cheerful pubs where the patrons sang, "On Ilkley Moor Bar't 'At." Sometimes we double- or triple-dated with her friends and mine.

She had a pixie sense of humor. Once, on a whim, she sprang atop a piece of masonry and posed for my camera like a statue, standing on one leg, arms outstretched, oblivious to onlookers who smiled indulgently at the antics of young love. She was decent, merry, sexy, and comfortable to be with.

It was only a matter of time, we knew, until I went home. I began visiting Bradford on week nights, taking an early afternoon train to join her after work. I never met her parents. We always spent the evening out, ending up around midnight in her mother's diminutive parlor, speaking in whispers and holding each other close on the sofa until it was 2 A.M. and I left on the dead run for my train.

Big boots clattering on the echoing cobblestones in the dead of a soft May night, racing downhill—*I've left it too late again!*—toward the railway station in the center of town. Train waiting on its familiar track, wheezing, hissing, in pools of yellow smoky light. Tired engine, tired old cars from heavy duty in a long war.

A few other sweaty airmen, puffing and flushed with passion like me, converge from their own assignations. We recognize one another and nod or mutter greetings. We sneak into first-class compartments if the trainman isn't looking. Sometimes he comes around, checks our third-class tickets, and boots us out. But he was young and in love once himself, and we still enjoy the cachet that the RCAF uniform has earned. So, often he lets us stay, although he knows what's going on. The whistle goes "PEEP," the train sidles out toward the Moors, and we lie back in first-class plush, dozing and dreaming that we are toffs.

Soon after dawn the train drops me at camp in time for a shower, a shave, and breakfast. I show up on morning parade red eyed but supremely happy. Only the young and strong could sustain such a pace.

June 4 was our last night. We whispered promises, and meant them. It was implied, without quite being said, that someday I would ask her to come to Canada, and she would come. Then I raced to catch the red-eye special back to base one last time, and heaved my kit bag aboard yet another truck one last time, to yet another train, bound for Southhampton.

Vera and I would correspond, briefly. Her letters would come to Shamrock with lipstick kisses imprinted on the back of the envelope, as was the fashion of the time. And I, temporarily back in the small-town fishbowl, would be embarrassed by my parents' insinuating glances (they never asked but were dying of curiosity) and the knowledge that the post office people noticed too.

More important: In the harsh clear light of civvy street came the certain knowledge that I had many things to do, things that had been postponed too long, and marriage was not one of them. Yorkshire and Vera would suddenly seem not merely an ocean away but a culture and time out of some distant past.

So I would be the one to end it, and to receive one last hurt and angry letter. And to wonder ever after: *Was I any better than the airman who left the German girl crying outside the Phönix Hotel?*

Chapter Fifteen

By the luck of the draw we sailed home on the *Aquitania*. The food and smell of the galley hadn't improved, but after crossing the North Sea on a small boat, nothing could make me seasick again. High on the topmost deck ("OUT OF BOUNDS to All Ranks") rode a distinguished shipmate: Anthony Eden, former foreign minister in the Churchill cabinet and future prime minister. From the clutter of uniforms below I snapped a picture of his handsome graying head and stored another scrap of British trivia to impress my father.

On June 12 we boarded the train at Halifax for the long last ride across our beautiful country. I cast nostalgic glances at Campbellton, and the perfect green fields of Quebec. One by one we peeled off for home: Mac MacLean and a host of others at Toronto, where little railway tributaries would carry some all over southern Ontario; Gabe at the Sault; Al Cooper at Winnipeg, Smitty bound for Edmonton, Jim Williams headed for Revelstoke.

We watched men transform as by magic from swashbucklers and lechers into model husbands and fiances. One, whose sexual exploits had been legendary in Uetersen, stepped out on a small-town–Ontario platform into the arms of a dazzling wife. Her chestnut hair hung in glossy waves; she wore a pale yellow summer frock with matching hat; she was surrounded by a giggling coterie of sisters (I supposed) and mother. Our man kissed her passionately (well aware of the cynical eyes on his back) and briskly hustled her out of our range. They walked off laughing, hand in hand. Being rid of my prewar illusions about fidelity, I wondered idly if *she* had been faithful to *him*.

Late one night the CPR mainliner paused sixty seconds to drop me, my kit bag, and my plywood suitcase at Chaplin. My father, brother, and Mister Adams with his car were waiting at the little darkened depot. In the blurring light of the vanishing coaches I grasped my brother's hand and hugged my father hard. Soon I was babbling, regaling them with my adventures. *But how can I ever tell you all of it, my family? I never will. It runs too deep.* My brother obligingly laughed at my jokes. My father grinned with pleasure, memories from the other war flickering through his eyes at the sound of my chatter. We were man to man now but we were never two veterans sharing confidences. His war and mine were far too different.

An hour later I was home, hugging my mother. She was not an effusive woman. *"Well,* Son!" she said, her face shining with relief. Then our torrent of happy talk poured out far into the night.

Shamrock's low profile reared against the moonlit sky: the three grain elevators, the post office, Rex Turner's garage, the two stores. Nothing seemed to have changed. It was snug, safe, familiar, dear—and *very* small. It was home. Saskatchewan would always be home. But now, after England and Paris and Brussels and Germany, I dimly sensed that I would leave it often and maybe forever. The world out there was beckoning.

It was over. What had I done? I had not visibly been at risk nor aided the war effort. At some expense to the Canadian taxpayers, I had volunteered and gone where I was told. In different circumstances, I might have made a worthy contribution. But in literal fact, I did not.

Once—the only time she ventured such a confidence—my mother said, choosing her words with care, "We're very proud of how you came through, Son, and didn't change."

She meant, of course, that I hadn't become uncouth, profane (at least in her presence), or riddled with unmentionable disease; that I seemed to have clung to the values they'd instilled in me. Which was essentially true, but I had changed far more than she knew. I came out of it the winner because of that rare opportunity to glimpse the world, and grow. I had shed bits of bigotry that, at the start, I didn't know were in me. I had found love and lost it, and survived. I'd learned the art of travel, and relished it. No longer was I agonizingly tongue-tied. Having come from a place where six was a crowd, I'd learned how to live and cope with men in groups. All of these were assets for living and for a future reporter who would sometimes find himself in strange rough places.

Now I wanted to get on with life. I was fired up. Enough of the meaningless orders and mindless waiting. Now *I* was in control. I knew for sure I could never be happy with farming or anything like it. The war had helped me and thousands of others break out of the trap of the Depression. It took a bite from my life—afterward, most of my contemporaries in education and jobs were three or four years younger—but it repaid me handsomely with a university education. My parents' dream had come true.

On July 16 those of us from the prairies reported to Winnipeg for discharge. Out at No. 5 Release Centre we lined up, waited, lined up, waited for the last time. There was a festive air among us. This was the last parade. I turned in the dog tags that had traveled in the bottom of my kit bag for nearly three years. (Lucky I wasn't blown to bits; they'd never have identified me.)

The MO gave us a final once-over. Teeth okay. Heart okay. No short-arm inspection, thank God. If any of us had VD the MO didn't want to know about it. Still a slight ringing in the left ear from a rifle range eighteen months before; it would be with me for life and no doctor would figure out why.

In three years my weight had soared from 125 pounds to a respectable 147 and my chest had expanded two inches to thirty-three. My pay had plateaued at the dizzying level of two dollars a day. Based on this and on my length of service, the air force gave me a cash gratuity of $421.57, to be meted out in five payments. Like most others I also received the RCAF Reserve button, the Canadian Volunteer Service Medal with clasp (commonly known as the Spam Medal, for time spent abroad eating Britain's ubiquitous canned meat), and the Victory Medal. All three were later lost.

At last we got down to our futures. One by one we sat down with RCAF counsellors. They were a caricature head-shrinker team. One sat silently in a corner throughout the interview, earnestly puffing the mandatory pipe and watching me unblinkingly for—I guessed—nervous tics and other signs of frailty. The other, a flight lieutenant named Palmer, quizzed me thoroughly but amiably. For the first time I felt that an officer was on my side. A friend next in line overheard them say after I'd left, "That boy will go places!" It was the nicest thing anybody had said about me in three years.

Nearly a lifetime later, I saw Palmer's full report: "Keen and alert type of airman, quiet, conscientious with outstanding learning and clerical ability. Has always been interested in newspaper work. Has worked on school and service papers. Did free lance writing for Regina *Leader-Post*. Plans to follow journalistic career and would appear to have all the necessary abilities to lead to success."

A few weeks later the Department of Veterans Affairs in Regina backed up the air force appraisal: "He is a quiet, very sincere young man . . . studious, conscientious and very well motivated for his proposed training. His pleasant personality, good health, mental alertness and resourcefulness should be valuable assets to his proposed career. He realizes the difficulties which he may encounter in an attempt to advance in the Journalistic field and is also giving some consideration to Law, Teaching, Social Service or Library Science." They granted me university tuition and sixty dollars a month allowance during the academic year and I was deeply grateful.

I left No. 5 Release Centre without a pang or backward glance. I was proud to have served in the Royal Canadian Air Force, but for me the war was neither so good nor so bad that I lived ever after on its memories. Some did. A friend in first-year university —ex–bomber pilot, intellectually brilliant but eyes pouchy and face gray from hard liquor and hard nights—burned out quickly. He could only drink, and relive the ugliness and the glory days.

Forty years later, some *still* talk of the war like an old love. For me, luckily, it was just a vivid episode. I did not see friends cut to bits by gunfire. I did not flounder gasping for life in an oily sea. I did not come home crippled. Could I ever know how those others feel?

Yet in the after years, as I matured, I sensed a kind of indebtedness—eloquently defined by a Lieutenant Donald Pearce of the North Nova Scotia Highlanders. Pearce kept a diary during the last fierce winter of fighting in Europe; it was published in 1965 under the title *Journal of War*. He survived when scores around him did not. When he was finally pulled out of the lines in March 1945, he wrote

> All my life I will be under the obligation of accomplishing something as a result of having lived through the war. Something tells me I must work hard, as if atoning for not being killed. I will doubtless outlive this feeling. But that will be because I have lost touch with the soldier's truth. Not to have been killed is unfashion-

131

able among those who are still dying. Not to have been wounded is something to do penance for.

It is not that there is anything particularly desirable about being killed; in itself, even a soldier's death is not precisely desirable. It is in not being killed that the strange obligation exists. I think of the splendid ones who have died, how splendid few will know. They have made it seem as if anything short of intense labor is trifling or shameful.

I suppose their smiling eyes, perpetually young and soldierly in memory now, will be the strict judges of my leisure forever. You cannot stare them out, or turn them aside with a sleepy look. They can exact anything. Tonight I have the feeling that they will make me work. It is owing. . . .

We all still owe them, especially those of us who were never in danger.

A last visit with Al Cooper at his Winnipeg home. A small slim man, he looked infinitely smaller now in his civilian clothes. He had been a friend for more than two years, but I never saw him again. Our friendship *was* real but we didn't share the life-and-death bond that drew former air crew back together again, year after year. Our reborn individualism was already leading us down different paths.

I saw it even in the way Smitty, Williams, and yet another new friend Frank Pollock dressed when we went to the Calgary Stampede for one last modest fling. Smitty blossomed out in a cowboy hat. Jim wore a leisure jacket, open shirt, and huge sunny grin. Pollock and I wore jackets and ties. We saw all the rodeo rides, drank a little beer, and said our goodbyes. We exchanged Christmas cards for a while but I never saw *them* again.

A Stampede carnie skinned me of forty dollars in five minutes —three weeks' air force pay—in the oldest con on earth: a shell game. I, who thought myself so worldly, so desperately wanted the prize, a typewriter, that I temporarily lost my wits.

There was enough gratuity money left over for a new brown tweed jacket and two loud neckties, predominantly red (I was allergic to blue for several years). I could hardly wait for autumn and the University of Saskatchewan. On my last day in Calgary a sidewalk photographer snapped my picture, walking the streets in my new finery.

I had the whole wide world ahead of me, and I was whistling.

Epilogue

. . . we're saying goodbye to them all
As back to the barracks we crawl
There'll be no promotion,
This side of the ocean
So cheer up, my lads, bless 'em all . . .

Brandon Manning Depot has vanished without a trace. A shopping center and liquor store stand in its place. In Moose Jaw the Douglas Block, home of the War Emergency Training Program, now has apartments upstairs and shops downstairs. If you look closely on sunny days, you will see the ghosts of jolly airmen lounging along its Main Street frontage, punching biceps and guzzling chocolate milk.

My old boarding house still stands on River Street East. Temple Gardens is gone but the Harwood Hotel remains, less grand than I remembered it but still a friendly oasis for shy country folk.

The Technical Training Station in St. Thomas reverted to its original role of mental institution after the war, but from the outside it is little changed. There's talk of naming it a historic site. The L&PS railway gave up passenger service in the 1950s but the rusting track remains.

Most of the airfields I knew were turned into civil aviation strips or farmers' fields. I once looked for traces of the Wombleton base, but found none among the Yorkshire fields. I never returned to Germany but Herb Gallifent visited a totally rebuilt Hamburg in 1980. He found only two recognizable landmarks: Bismarck's statue and the Hotel Phönix, the latter with a "Pizza" sign above its marquee.

Sam Glassford, whom I never saw after the war, worked for

Ontario Hydro and died too young of cancer in 1972. The former Constance Macnab still lives in the United States. Her Belfast accent has given way to a southern drawl. Her marriage fell apart many years ago. Her spirit and humor remain bright but she works too hard at a factory job, and deserves better. We looked each other up again in 1980, with fragile hopes on both our parts. But some things, once broken, can never be repaired.

Gallifent returned to Hamilton after the war and has worked there for Westinghouse most of his life. Eldon Fairburn works in Vancouver with the audio-visual department of a school system. William Arnold Steppler of New Westminster operated his own pharmacy for many years and is now semiretired. Reg Starks is a prosperous farmer at Naicam, Saskatchewan. Joe Fink, still at Plunkett, has retired from farming and drives a school bus. In Regina, Roy Bien lives in semiretirement from a job with the Saskatchewan Liquor Board. Bill McVean has been a popular broadcaster on CFRB, Toronto, for twenty-five years.

In seeking them out for this book—not without trepidation, and in most cases for the first time in forty years—I realized why we were friends so long ago. We were different people with different dreams and after the war, like most ex–servicemen, we went our various ways. Yet I rediscovered in them the same humor and integrity and generosity of spirit that once drew us together.

In the end, they are my best and most enduring memory of the war.